# Praise for *Meaningful Alignment*

"*Meaningful Alignment* is a must read for those who have to deal with difficult situations or discussions, whether professional or personal. It takes a balanced, nuanced approach to problem-solving through thoughtful conversation and collaboration, all in the spirit of building and preserving lasting relationships. Our entire team has applied this approach, and it works extremely well. It's been an absolute game-changer for us; you don't want to miss out!"

—BILL DUNCAN, Global Head Hilton - All Suites, Focused Service, Owner Relations Category

"Alignment is a powerful word. It requires trust, respect, and transparency. Each of these requires an uncommon willingness and ability to converse. Most of us have great conversations only by accident. This story will not only resonate with you but also give you insight into how you might have great conversations on demand. Everyone that cares about you will benefit."

—PAUL AXTELL, author of
*Ten Powerful Things to Say to Your Kids*

"Through engaging story-telling, *Meaningful Alignment* reveals how we can overcome obstacles in our business and personal relationships by helping the reader to recognize the difference between various personality types (including their own) and their distinct modes of communication. *Meaningful Alignment* provides thoughtful and actionable approaches to handling conflict, managing emotions and enhancing one's communication skills. A must-read for anyone who wants to achieve alignment in their relationships — both personally and professionally."

—JILL OLANDER, Executive Vice President
Human Resources, Park Hotel & Resorts

"Handling emotions effectively is an indispensable leadership skill in business today. *Meaningful Alignment* brilliantly paves the way to successfully navigate high-stakes conversations with greater emotional resiliency. A must-read for our times."

—STEPHAN M. MARDYKS, Founder and CEO of
Wisdom Destinations and coauthor of *Quantum Negotiation*

"Knowledge is no longer enough. The huge changes ahead in most aspects of our lives necessitates the need to be able to develop emotionally intelligent interactions with the new, the never before and the altering of human relationships. A timely and important topic. Steinbrecher, as usual, shows us the way."

—Futurist DAVID HOULE

"A quick read with a powerful message. *Meaningful Alignment* hits the mark to bolster success in every aspect of business and life."

—KARIN HURT, Co-author *Winning Well: A Manager's Guide to Getting Results—Without Losing Your Soul*

"Bravo! *Meaningful Alignment* champions the message that by building a healthy reserve of emotional resilience, you are able to create — and maintain — rewarding relationships for the long-term."

—MARSHALL GOLDSMITH is the *New York Times* #1 bestselling author of *Triggers, Mojo,* and *What Got You Here Won't Get You There*

"*Meaningful Alignment* is an eye-opener for all successful people because emotional resilience is an intentional skill which gives you the power to choose happiness."

—DR. JOHN IZZO, Bestselling author of *The Purpose Revolution, The Five Thieves of Happiness, The Five Secrets You Must Discover before You Die* and *Stepping Up*

"At a time when we feel more inundated than ever by a constant flow of stress, conflict and over-communication, *Meaningful Alignment* is a timely and effective tool for significantly improving our most critical relationships at work and, more importantly, in our lives away from the office."

—John W. Robinson III,
Chief Executive Officer, Aaron's, Inc.

"*Meaningful Alignment* allows us to see clearly, that the world outside of us is simply a reflection of the world within us. A very timely body of work."

—Mark C. Crowley, author of *Lead From The Heart: Transformational Leadership For The 21st Century*

# MEANINGFUL ALIGNMENT

# MEANINGFUL ALIGNMENT

## MASTERING EMOTIONALLY INTELLIGENT INTERACTIONS
### *at* **WORK** *and in* **LIFE**

SUSAN STEINBRECHER
AND ROBERT SCHAEFER, PH.D.

WITH JOANNE MOYLE

FOREWORD *by* DAVID M.R. COVEY

For more information about the Meaningful Alignment program:
www.meaningfulalignment.com

ISBN 978-0-578-40684-8

# CONTENTS

# ACKNOWLEDGMENTS

IT IS WITH HUMILITY AND heartfelt thanks that we share with you the phenomenal job that Joanne Moyle did on this book. Her tireless and selfless service has instilled this work with a sense of commitment and passion rarely found in this world. This book would simply not exist without Joanne.

We would also like to thank Jill Armstrong for all of her effort and dedication to helping make this book the best that it could be.

To our editor, Laura Barth, who helped take an excellent draft to a level that was beyond expectation, and to Stewart Williams, our graphic designer, for his insight and creativity.

To Stephan Mardyks for his ongoing wisdom, advice, and support.

Finally, thanks to you, the reader, for your interest, for taking the time to read this work and for your sincere desire to have more meaningful and impactful relationships in your life.

# FOREWORD

THIS BOOK HAS COME FORTH at a defining moment in history. No one would disagree that at this particular juncture, we as a culture are struggling in our communication with one another. This is significant. Without the ability to communicate, particularly during high-stakes interactions, our relationships suffer and our businesses or careers can derail.

In my work over the years, first with FranklinCovey and now in my own company SMCOV, I have learned that self-discovery and self-management are two critical elements to a fulfilling career—and to a successful life. It's clear to me that we, as leaders, parents, friends, and members of the community, must strive to model the behavior we wish to see in others. The old "do as I say, not as I do" mentality is wearing thin. It's time to step up to the plate and become more proactive in finding ways to build upon our capacity to communicate with more composure and finesse, and empower others to do the same.

Why did you pick up this book? Maybe you just finished a disjointed conversation with a family member or you had a heated discussion with a co-worker. You might be feeling frustrated and unable to discern why these unpleasant interactions keep coming to the forefront, and you are unable to pinpoint the cause. Does it feel like you are continually trying to keep up with the demands of life while attempting to preserve equanimity with your employees, superiors or spouse? Are you searching for a way to enhance employee loyalty and increase productivity?

You may find some answers here.

Simultaneously practical and inspirational, the Meaningful Alignment program was created by management consulting firm Steinbrecher and Associates, Inc. to address these thorny issues effectively. Packed with real-world advice and leadership wisdom, their book dives deep beneath the surface of everyday problems. It offers help in an easy-to-read story format that effortlessly teaches the reader how to handle the toughest conversations. These are not just cookie-cutter methods to improve communication. Meaningful Alignment is a holistic system that gets to the very core of why we are often suffering in our relationships and interactions with one another and offers help in finding a better way.

DAVID M. R. COVEY
CEO of SMCOV & Co-Author of *Trap Tales – Outsmarting the 7 Hidden Obstacles to Success*

# INTRODUCTION

THE DIFFICULTY WE ALL FACE when effectively communicating with coworkers, customers, neighbors, and even family members, is a very real and painful social problem. Our lives have become so immersed in smart technology that contacting one another at any hour of the day or night has become the new normal. In fact, our ability to connect through multiple mediums has never been easier—or more powerful. Unfortunately, this omnipresent connectivity often fails to facilitate encounters that are meaningful and personally rewarding. In the same way that information does not equate to knowledge, and followers do not equate to friends, communication does not equate to meaningful understanding.

Rather than serving as a conduit for connection, our universal accessibility has created the exact opposite: disconnection. Take, for example, the workplace. We live amid a sweeping trend that confuses frequent communication efforts with effective collaboration, wherein the allocation of work is intelligently based on our priorities, capacities and personal growth. Throughout the workplace, we often mistake signal with noise and productivity with busyness. As a consequence, many people are routinely lulled into a state of overproduction, saying yes to every person, project and meeting request. The ego-driven desire many feel to be the standout superstar at work has backfired, generating an enormous cost to the teams they sincerely desire to serve.

A recently concluded eight-year study of twenty organizations revealed data findings that collaborative time demands have increased by 50% over the past decade, and individuals who work in knowledge-based or leadership roles are now spending more than 85% of their time managing the interpersonal communication demands of their job (Cross, Madden and Taylor 2018). Although it is easy for us to blame our ever-expanding work week and saturated inboxes on things beyond our immediate control, the real enemy we must confront is ourselves.

When we do engage in face-to-face communication, many of us lack the tools required to tackle the difficult subject and to engage the difficult person. Despite the glowing promise of the Information Age making us more productive, we've lost what matters the most in the process: the art of conversation.

Life in the Information Age may also be contributing to disengagement in our personal lives. According to a 2012 study by the Stanford Center on Longevity, baby boomers (age 55+) are more isolated and less socially engaged than their predecessors were just twenty years earlier. This includes having far fewer meaningful interactions with their spouses, weaker ties with family members and friends, fewer connections with neighbors and less involvement with their local communities (Carstensen 2016). The biggest concern associated with these findings, is the significant, long-term health risks that this behavior is creating—most notably, to our life expectancy. Although the explanation for this trend has many causal aspects to consider, one inescapable contributing factor is that our connection to technology overrides our connection to one another. We believe this growing sense of isolation is not limited to boomers (who were the focus of the Stanford research) but includes the generations following them.

In our executive coaching work, we have used the assessment

of emotional intelligence to help increase self-regulation strategies and improve the quality of relationships that our clients have at work and at home. Over the past twenty-five years, there have been many books and articles written on emotional intelligence (or EI), many of them quite outstanding. These books cover a wide range of topics, such as why EI is important, the underpinning theories of EI, and whether it is a cognitive ability or a personality trait. Some books offer the reader a collection of constructive habits to adopt and valuable life tips to practice, aimed at helping readers improve their emotional intelligence. These are useful to some extent, but we came to a realization some time ago that none of the books we had read or were recommending to people over the years were helping them to significantly shift the social dimension of their lives in a meaningful and enduring way. As a result, we have focused our initial research for this book, and the dialogue model for Meaningful Alignment, on the impact that our emotional intensity and sensitivity have on behavior, above and beyond the scope of emotional intelligence.

Consider for a moment how emotional intelligence is measured on most assessments. Results reflect a person's best intentions and highest and best sense of self. After all, when asked, most people will tell you that they prefer acts of empathy and cooperation to those of selfishness and distrust. Most people also recognize that being cool under pressure is a more desirable trait than a tendency to shut down or run away from social difficulty. But the inner world of our affect (our inner world of feeling and sensing) in real time paints a much different picture of our external behavior.

When we are faced with a high-stress, high-impact situation, initial sensory signals are sent to the thalamus, which functions as a signal receptor and "relay switch" of sorts to different areas of our brain. One important neural pathway travels directly from the thalamus to the amygdala in the limbic system, which is the epicenter of our fight-or-flight response. This pathway is far stronger and more sensitive in some people than it is for others. Furthermore, the conditioned patterns that trigger the fight-or-flight response will also vary greatly from person to person. This is not easily captured during the calm of taking an online assessment of our own emotional intelligence. Each person is born with a unique arousal baseline mixed with a lifelong history of trial and error experience. This has serious implications for how and why each of us decides to engage or avoid people at critical moments.

For executive leaders, the development of skills and abilities associated with managing and controlling responses to stressful moments will ultimately determine whether or not their inherent emotional intelligence can be leveraged to maximum effect. More directly, it will likely determine the trajectory of their career. For this reason, the Meaningful Alignment program was developed to build skills that help people to self-regulate, to take full advantage of their emotional intelligence by recognizing and respecting the power of their underlying affect intensity, and to manage the unique set of dialogue styles that predict what their strongest response triggers will be. Finally, we focus on preparation and performance—that is, how to have conversations that lead to Meaningful Alignment! Self-discovery is the prerequisite for self-improvement.

Meaningful Alignment is challenging work, but it is also extremely rewarding and liberating. Success in this key area of life requires self-determination and tenacity. Ultimately, Meaningful Alignment requires us to build our resilience, expand our options for self-regulation and increase the competence necessary to rework our learned social responses and replace them with wiser, more effective techniques, including a focus on mindfulness, gratitude and emotional self-care. These practices create greater levels of trust, appreciation and collaborative efforts that lead to deep commitment and mutual understanding.

We believe that the social problems we are facing can be overcome one relationship at a time, beginning with the relationship we have with ourselves. It is only when we engage in the inner work of reflection and the outer work of skill development that we will be capable of effective collaboration at work and at home and able to realize lasting happiness with the most important people in our lives.

The story you are about to read illustrates some of the ageless truths that prevail throughout our lives. It is also our story—the story behind our research and, ultimately, why we developed the Meaningful Alignment program.

You may wonder why we decided to write a fictional story about Carl, the protagonist of our book, instead of simply presenting our research on Meaningful Alignment.

Storytelling is undeniably one of the most potent forms of human communication and significant connection. Throughout history, since people began speaking in the earliest form of language, we have been telling stories to one another to help us make sense of the world we live in. Why the tides ebb and flow, why the moon waxes and wanes, and the reason for changing seasons—as well as the interpretations of innumerable human experiences. Stories help us understand the human condition, and they are an essential part of our day-to-day communication.

We are hardwired to receive information via storytelling; gaining information through a story dramatically increases our ability to understand and retain that knowledge. The stories we tell shape our identity as individuals and help us make sense of our world as a society. We are, all of us, an endlessly unfolding narrative, the heroes of our own unique story.

We are excited to share this journey of self-realization through the fictional tale of Carl and the people central to his life. We believe you may find some commonalities in the power of Carl's journey, and we hope that it may lead you to explore ways to find meaningful connections and more gratifying communication in your own life.

# CHAPTER ONE

I*T WAS A BEAUTIFUL SPRING DAY*. *The air was fresh with new life. Carl was on an empty road, driving…just driving. Leaving the city behind. Soon, he found himself on a lonely back road with gently sloping farm fields and woodland on either side. He rolled down the window and took in a few deep breaths. The air was sweet and fragrant, and the smell of the earth awakening was all around him. The road was empty. He allowed himself to relax and release the strain of life. He felt alive and free.*

*As he drove with no destination in mind, something urged him ever forward. A hazy sadness overtook him, an undefined longing tugging at him, beckoning to him. He decided to simply*

◆

*let it go, to quiet his mind and be in the moment. He opened himself to the beauty of creation. He felt a sense of connection to everything, as though the rhythm of the universe flowed through him. He slowed to a stop on the dusty dirt road to take it all in. Pristine evergreens flanked the bends of the meandering route. He looked around at the tall pines. The peaceful breeze set them gently swaying, while birdsong punctuated the sound of the wind through the trees...*

*Wheee... Wheeee... Wheeeeee...*

The alarm sounded like a siren wailing throughout the room, leaping out from the corners, echoing through his head. *What a dream...!* He could still feel the crisp coolness of the air and smell the earthy pines as he drove that winding road. And the sense of freedom—he wished it could go on forever.

Carl sat up in a sleepy stupor, dangling his feet over the edge of the bed.

*I guess I shouldn't have had that third beer last night. Or was it four?* A few drinks always helped relieve the unremitting sense of apprehension that he felt day after day. Dread owned him, it seemed. And right in this moment, it was pushing against him like an invisible weight, attempting to shove him back to bed and back into that beautiful dream. He reached over and turned off the alarm.

◆

"Older and wiser." That was how his friends had teased him at his birthday get-together last week.

*Not a chance...*

At forty-seven, Carl felt lost at sea. He never awoke refreshed and ready to greet the day anymore. Everything ached, and his body felt like an anchor. No question, he had issues. His doctor had read him the riot act at his yearly physical. "You're at least twenty pounds overweight, Carl, and I don't like the look of your blood work," he'd cautioned. "Your cholesterol is too high, as is your sugar, and you have high inflammatory biomarkers, which all point to imminent cardiovascular issues. These results, combined with the fact that your blood pressure is borderline high, are indications that you need to change your lifestyle—and soon." Dr. Ennis had a way of looking right through him.

Carl had not been surprised by his doctor's warnings—he just didn't feel right. Yet instead of taking action, he'd settled into a comfortable state of suspended disbelief. Part of him sensed there was something waiting for him—something earth-shattering—over the next horizon. He felt ashamed that his current lifestyle was so far removed from that of the guy who'd worked out at the gym three to four times a week and had always been up on the latest healthy cooking trends.

Cooking was creative; he loved putting together wholesome meals and feeling proud that he knew the breakdown of every nutrient, calorie and gram of fat. It was also fun. But that was when he actually had the time and the energy for it. It was stressful knowing he wasn't healthy. Maybe that was what was keeping him awake at night…

Most nights, after waking several times, he couldn't get back to sleep, worrying about work or family issues. Last night had been no different—a write-off.

*Ugh…all I want to do is lie in bed for the rest of the day.*

Carl looked at the notebook on the bedside table and flipped it open to the first few pages. He remembered that he had scrawled something in it before bed. *I can't talk to my son anymore. It's like he's on a different planet. His phone has become an appendage. How do I get through to him? I hope it's not drugs…*

Carl was worried about his only child. At thirteen, Sam seemed sullen and antisocial. Every time Carl tried to talk to him, Sam would clam up and go back to his phone. Carl couldn't talk to his wife about it, but he knew she was very concerned as well. Maria was so high-strung these days, he was sure her blood pressure was affected too—her reactions were so severe. He didn't want to talk to his friends about his son either. They would just try to joke him out of it and tell him he was imagining things. Besides, he wasn't even sure what was wrong—so how would he explain it? There were times that he felt so powerless, so ineffective as a parent. He had to do something.

Several months ago, after a major project at work blew up, Carl had seen the notebook in the desk drawer of the study. He'd opened it and immediately begun making brief observations about things that were bothering him. He hid it in a drawer and grabbed it whenever the mood struck—usually late at night after he'd had a couple of drinks to relax. It couldn't hurt. Writing was something Carl had enjoyed throughout college— he'd even written a song for Maria when they were dating. But it was something he had given up on long ago, before life had become so rushed and unbelievably thorny.

*No more time for reflection...*

He jumped up to get in the shower.

◆

Maria was late, as usual. She got up at least forty-five minutes before Carl, but somehow she was always scrambling. In her rushing she became somewhat clumsy. "Darn it, Carl," she shouted, "why can't you clean up after yourself?" A beer bottle

◆

crashed to the floor. *Here she goes again*. He sighed.

Last night's argument was still bothering him. Maria had made another "big speech." Something about the fact that he didn't pay attention to her and that she felt ignored. It was always the same thing, over and over again. What did she expect? Work was so stressful, and their finances were strained. And now these issues with their son... Carl was simultaneously drained and dejected.

"You're either on your phone or glued to the TV," she'd begun.

"Oh, come on, you're exaggerating," Carl had countered.

"No, I'm not. I feel like you don't care. You never listen to what I say anyway, so what's the point."

"You're overreacting! Let's face it, no matter what I do you're never satisfied."

"Why are we even together?"

More and more these days, Maria concluded their arguments with that ominous question. Their fights had become a never-ending script of negativity, played out until one of them stormed from the room or shut down. Carl felt their marriage might be at the point of no return. He worried there was no way out of this mess, and he was sick and tired of sleeping in the guest room after they quarreled.

Carl reflected on their life together when they were first married. Life had seemed so much simpler then. They were young and in love, living in a small two-bedroom apartment in a house in Glendonwynne Village, a leafy older neighborhood west of the city. Glendonwynne was teeming with great markets, restaurants and a brand-new community center. Carl and Maria would meet at the apartment each day after work at six-thirty, go for a quick workout, cook dinner together or go out to eat at one of the local places that catered to health-conscious young professionals. They were always lively eateries, full of friendly staff and delicious food.

Once Maria became pregnant with Sam, though, things began to change. Carl and Maria realized that within nine months they would quickly outgrow their cozy apartment and felt it was time to buy into the housing market. The problem was, the market had experienced a recent upswing and prices were almost out of reach—but they both believed if they didn't jump in they'd regret it.

They purchased a "fixer-upper" further west of the city and hired a contractor to do some cosmetic renovations. One thing led to another as the contractor unearthed some insidious and costly structural issues: the roof needed replacing, the plumbing was cast iron and leaking in several places, and there was some mold inside the ceiling of the front hallway that had to be removed by a team of experts. The bills started piling up. On top of that, the city had begun harmonizing zoning by-laws across several municipalities, and building permits were delayed. The house sat empty, gutted to the studs, for months.

While the house was still under construction, Maria gave birth to Sam and the couple came home to the apartment. They were in a state of "baby bliss." The young parents were so happy, they didn't care that it was cramped and getting more and more cluttered with toys and other baby gear every day.

*We were so close back then...* Carl recalled the times he would cook while Maria fed the baby, and then they would eat dinner by candlelight or in front of a romantic movie together while Sam slept soundly in the bassinette.

Almost seventeen months after they had purchased the house, it was finally move-in ready. The house was unrecognizable from its former self. There were big windows in every room, as well as a lovely custom-designed kitchen with marble countertops, and three bright and spacious bedrooms—including a master with a walk-in closet and a walk out to a deck. It was heaven on earth compared to their former cramped quarters, but the bills were utterly staggering. Carl tried to reassure Maria. "It will all work out, you'll see," he promised her. "We'll find the money to pay for everything, no worries."

The next several years were so nerve-wracking. Carl couldn't remember much about them, apart from the angst he'd felt in the pit of his stomach. He'd realized they owed far more to the contractor than he had originally planned for, and they had already used up all their savings and their "emergency fund" for renovations. Forced to borrow from family members to finish paying for everything, Carl had also been stunned to realize they needed to secure a whopping line of credit that would be impossible to pay down unless something changed drastically. The only thing he considered a saving grace was that home values in the area continued to escalate.

Nightly panic attacks had plagued Carl as he'd thought about what he and his wife had gotten themselves into. And a new baby... He tried his best to let go of the negativity he felt over what had happened. He had felt duped by an overpriced contractor, some very bad luck, and was ashamed of his own colossal hubris and ignorance.

*How did we get here...?*

◆

Carl hurriedly got ready for work. The I-75 was getting pretty nasty in the morning. Sam was still sitting at the dining room table lingering over a bowl of cereal while Carl was standing, eating over the sink, gulping down a slice of toast and a glass of juice.

"Son, you're going to be late for school again. By the way, where is your mother?" Sam was glued to his phone, as usual. "She left," was all he mumbled, without looking up.

*She always leaves for work without saying goodbye... That stings, especially after last night. She's either yelling at me or ignoring me.*

Carl merged into traffic on the I-75; it was bumper to bumper—the Chicago-area morning rush hour was so brutal. He was thinking about the extensive list of things he needed to accomplish at work, sipping on his coffee from a travel mug emblazoned with the words *Life's a Beach*. Yeah, right, he thought. There were days he just wanted to throw that mug out the window. He almost resented the memories it held for him when he compared it to his current reality. That unforgettable, carefree vacation with Maria and Sam in the Cayman Islands... What a trip. The natural surroundings, the beach, and the spectacular hotel... He couldn't even remember the last time he'd had a vacation like that. To add insult to injury, this was the third year in a row he had to cancel the family vacation because of a production issue. And this one was a complete disaster.

The client had been livid and threatened to pull their business. They were one of the top design firms in the country, and the project was very high profile. The architect for the design firm had specified a unique product—multi-colored dichroic glass for a hotel in Dubai from the architectural division of the company Carl worked for, Solar Glass. It would be such a jewel in Solar's crown—a real showpiece that would encourage further referrals. The budget of 2.8 million would have made Carl's entire year, not to mention garnered him a substantial bonus. But the stars had not lined up. The whole project had been beleaguered from the beginning. They'd had no business accepting the contract for the venture in the first place, but the plant manager, Jake, had said he had it all figured out and to trust him—that it wouldn't be a problem. Jake had seemed so confident. He'd explained that he had done something similar in the past with a laminating material that was so close to the dichroic, and he'd insisted it would work. Carl had signed off on the project after getting Jake to agree to consult engineering on a daily basis, and he'd neglected to do further research on the new process or ask for additional proof they could deliver. For jobs of this scope, he usually did far more due diligence— but he hadn't come close to his sales projections for the year. And so far, this year was no different. It was all about making targets, and besides, Carl was tired of doing all the heavy lifting—and had simply accepted Jake's explanation of the new process.

Then the trouble had begun. The recipe for the lamination did not take into account the shrinkage of the material—it was not engineered to take the heat of the laminating process and so was not produced according to specifications for exterior cladding. The stunning luminescent glass looked absolutely flawless once complete and ready to be packed in a shipping container bound for the Port of Jebel Ali. But by the time it arrived, the general contractor was in a state of panic; the dichroic film had shrunk inside the glass and was completely ruined. As vice president of sales, Carl was on the hook to determine a resolution. It all had to be redone and was late to site by over eight weeks. Solar had to pay penalties for not completing on time—including wages for every day the crew was on site waiting for the material—plus the cost to remake the glass. They lost the entire budget of the project—and then some. Not to mention the client. What a circus.

There was no way Carl could ever relax and let go. Lately he feared that if he was able to get away and take a vacation, someone at the office—like the new director of marketing, Karen—might usurp his efforts and try to bad-mouth him. Karen *seemed* OK, but the incessant questioning and nonstop discussion about all the changes she wanted to implement were making him crazy. She claimed to have a "better way" of doing everything, it seemed. What really inflamed Carl the most was that everyone liked her. Granted, she had a way of charming people—she got along with everybody. Maybe she knows the owner or someone in his family, he thought. Carl could sense somehow that Karen felt he was too set in his ways, but she didn't show it. She always tried to make him feel part of the team, including him in her weekly brainstorming sessions, and going out of her way to solicit his opinion about everything. But at a gut level, he still mistrusted her motives.

Karen had met with Carl privately one afternoon in her office to deliver her official laundry list. "Carl, the company website needs to be revamped," she'd asserted. "I'd love to hear your ideas on how we can make it better—together." She'd gone on, "I've also had a look at your sales materials and feel they are a little outdated. Don't you think they need a bit of a facelift? Were you happy with the original production?"

Carl had resented her questions and felt she was insulting his taste. After all, he was the one who had hired the people to help him with the website and printed materials that were currently in place. "I was hoping we could work together to develop a better follow-up program with customers," Karen had gone on enthusiastically, "and I was even thinking someone on your team could host web-based seminars for visitors to the website to obtain information on products more proficiently."

What audacity! As if I have time for all that, he thought. The pressure was always on. It was just too much some days. He felt the heat rising to his face and rolled down the window to get some air.

*It's always something…*

Carl turned on the radio to distract him from his thoughts. Music had a way of calming him. As he turned up the volume, he heard the announcer interrupt the programming. "Breaking news. A twenty-year-old student has fatally shot two and seriously wounded at least five more students as well as several staff members at Oakbrook University. First responders arrived at the scene thirty minutes ago, and the unidentified man had turned the gun on himself, taking his own life. Oakbrook is now under lockdown, and we will be bringing you updates as the scene unfolds."

How can this be happening yet again? Carl thought. What drives someone to do this? What sort of a world do we live in where we have to worry about sending our kids to school every day? What if that ever happened to Sam? Carl felt tears welling up, but fear and anger quickly overtook his sadness. He was dumbfounded.

Carl felt his heart pumping as he maneuvered through the rush hour traffic. He had to get to work. He needed to speak to Jake. There was no way the day could start on any other level before he had that conversation. Jake had no sense of urgency, and Carl feared yet another project was about to head south because of his ineptitude. Some days Carl felt so frustrated. Just about everyone he worked with at Solar—especially Jake—was useless.

Just as he was about to merge onto the off-ramp a driver darted across three lanes of traffic, cutting him off. He jumped. *That idiot!*

*Just breathe…*

# CHAPTER TWO

IT WAS A STRANGE MORNING. Two days earlier, a cold front had plunged down courtesy of a tempestuous artic mass that had descended from Canada, once more kissing the trees with a white blessing. "It's almost April," Carl muttered to himself. The weather had remained unseasonably cold, and Carl was still remembering that forty-eight hours earlier he had lost a ferocious battle with a snowbank. He and Sam had tried to shovel as much as they could, but they had given in after several hours, dog-tired. There were piles of snow everywhere, rapidly melting, transforming into jumbled puddles of icy slush.

As he pulled into the parking lot of Solar Glass at 8:45, Carl noticed the ice still clinging to the branches of the trees outside his office building. As he stepped out of his car and turned back to lock it, he observed the bumper that was slackly affixed to his quarter panel with Mammoth tape. There was no way he was going to give those pirates at the body shop over a thousand dollars to fix it. Yet one more reason to feel bitter about what Jake had done to obliterate his expectations of a bonus.

Lately, Carl incessantly put a price tag on every little detail of his life. Gone was the promise of the annual financial cushion he had waited for and counted on. He couldn't rid himself of the guilt he felt each time he used his credit card, knowing full well he would have a hard time paying it down. Maria wondered what was going on. Every time she suggested they eat at a restaurant he protested. "But, Carl, I'm tired!" she objected. "Why don't you make dinner then? And, by the way, since when do you not like eating out? You used to look forward to it."

*Since my credit card has neared its limit and I have no bonus to pay it down.*

Carl desperately wanted to come clean with Maria, but things were already so tenuous at home he would simply make an unimpressive excuse. His wife knew something was up—she just couldn't put her finger on it.

◆

Carl's heart began to pump harder as he walked through the west parking lot doors. He knew he had to speak to Jake before the meeting and rushed into the building, running up three flights of stairs. Once he got to the top, he realized not only was he huffing and puffing as he hit the third floor, but he was sweating profusely. He pulled off his jacket as he pushed open the heavy glass doors and saw that Jake and Ines had already gathered in the conference room, their heads lowered in what appeared to be a very involved discussion. Carl felt a lump in his throat.

*Oh great, that's all I need. The president of the company is listening to the person responsible for this awful mess. I'm being set up.*

Carl stepped into the room and thumped his travel mug on the table. Why had Ines and Jake started without him?

"I thought we called this meeting for 9:00 a.m.? Jake, I need to speak to you first about the latest update regarding the digital print on glass project for Truit Gas headquarters." He looked around. "Where is everyone else?"

"Carl, if you could just hold off…I thought we could take this opportunity to discuss the Dubai project first. I need to get a better handle on what happened during the lead-up to delivery," Ines explained.

"I think you'd better ask Jake to answer that one, Ines." Carl knew he was being a little antagonistic, but he didn't care. He'd *had it.* The fury was spiraling deep into his chest. Carl remained standing, holding on to the back of a chair with both hands, lifting it up and down almost imperceptibly.

*What I would give to throw this chair at Jake right now!*

He turned to address Ines. "From the get-go, this guy said he had it all under control," Carl admonished. "I kept asking about the engineering of this glass, and he said it wasn't a problem. When I asked him to prove to me that he had done his due diligence with engineering on the dichroic film for exterior use, he just waved me off and said, 'You do your job, and I'll do mine.' After a while, I just gave up!"

"That's not true at all, Carl," Jake argued. "Many times I came to you with the plans, and you kept saying, 'I thought you said you could handle it.' You didn't seem to want to hear if we had any issues, so I tried to deal with everything on my own. So please don't make it sound as if it's all my fault."

"Then whose fault is it?" Carl shot back.

"No one's…or if anything, it's engineering."

"You know, Jake, you've got problems," Carl said, each word coming out angrier than the preceding one. "I don't even know where to start."

Jake felt ready to pounce. He'd remained silent to Carl's finger-pointing too long. "Yes, I have problems—problems with you!"

"No, your issues are of a very different nature. You take on things and say you can handle them, when in reality you are nowhere near equipped to. You lied to me. You lied to Ines, here. You lied to all of us."

Several of the employees that were expected in the 9:00 a.m. meeting were hurriedly making their way down to the conference room, but they stopped dead in the hallway. Carl's voice could be heard coming from the meeting room into other parts of the office, seemingly bouncing off the exposed metal ventilation in the ceiling. The argument became so heated, they began to peek around the corner to catch a glimpse of what was happening through the glass walls, while others gathered near the conference room and began to watch, frozen in a moment of disbelief and uneasiness. They exchanged furtive glances but didn't dare enter the room or utter a word.

Ines was stunned. *How did it come to this? This is way out of hand.* There had been sporadic conflicts between Carl and Jake in the past but nothing this serious. "Stop! Both of you, just *stop!*"

Carl was swearing at Jake under his breath as Ines noticed

the onlookers outside the glass, so she lowered her voice, carefully enunciating her words through clenched teeth. "I know there's a lot of tension between the two of you over what happened with this project"—Ines spoke slowly and deliberately—"but I cannot condone this behavior. I think we need to discuss this in the privacy of my office. Would you both follow me please?"

As the conference room doors opened, Ines addressed the employees waiting outside. "I'm sorry, everyone, today's meeting will have to be postponed. I will send you an internal message with a new time slot."

The two men followed Ines into her office. She asked them to sit down and then offered them each a glass of water.

"Let's just take a breath for a moment, shall we? I have a few things to say, and I'd appreciate it if you wouldn't interject while I'm speaking."

Ines Pellichero had been president of Solar for eight years, and in all that time, she had never witnessed such hostility. Things had been on such an even keel for many years, and now it felt as though the relationship between two of the most crucial members of her team was fraught with problems, and it was affecting the entire company.

Ines began, "The way I see it is you are *both* to blame. Carl,

I don't think you exercised enough care and attention with this project, and your follow-up was either not documented well or it was non-existent. Jake, you were overconfident in your ability to do this on your own—based on a past project that was not comparative in scale to this one—and it should be said that you required additional intervention from engineering but did not seek it."

Carl felt temporarily vindicated.

"You both made some costly mistakes—but blaming each other won't solve anything, and it certainly won't make our money back." Ines went on, "Jake, I need you to do a post-mortem report on the dichroic project. Does a week from today sound doable?"

"Yes, no problem," Jake replied sheepishly.

"Jake, I'd like to speak to Carl privately now. We'll talk later."

As Jake got up to leave he shot a disparaging glance at Carl, and he grunted slightly as he knocked against Carl's chair on the way out.

Ines sat down next to Carl. "Carl, you really lost control in there. It was pretty astonishing to me that you got so heated—so quickly."

"Ines, I know," Carl began, "I've had a really bad month since all of this blew up, and I just can't get through to Jake.

He blames me for all his mistakes. And his people speak to me like I'm some sort of know-nothing fat cat and just ignore me when I ask them for project updates. Honestly, I think his department needs a total overhaul." Carl could still feel his heart pumping wildly.

"I think your issues with Jake have gone on for quite some time—even before this one," Ines observed. "I've noticed that in the past year or so, a relatively conflict-free relationship has changed dramatically. You began sitting apart from each other in meetings and blatantly trying to avoid one another in the office or at company functions. There seems to have been some sort of misunderstanding between you that has snowballed into suspicion of each other's motives, not to mention outright animosity. From my perspective, Carl, there are some issues to deal with—not just for the two of you but for you, individually, as well."

This train is going way off the rails, thought Carl. And why is she putting the blame on me?

"You know, I believe I have an idea that can help you," Ines said thoughtfully. "I think it would do you a world of good to work with an executive coach. A coach could offer unbiased, expert advice on your difficulties at work and may also be able to help you come to grips with your resentment and anger over what transpired." Ines knew there was more to Carl's behavior than met the eye and had a feeling there were personal issues to deal with, but she felt all of that could be best explored with a professional. "I worked with a coach myself about five years ago. Honestly, it's the best thing I ever did for myself and for my career. I only wish I had done it sooner."

Ines had appreciated the productive experience of working with a coach—it had helped her build a more solid foundation and move past a number of issues that were holding her back. She'd also been empowered to solidify her goals so she could realize her future.

"Oh, I don't think so. Look, I realize I was really inappropriate in there," Carl refuted, "but a coach? That's not necessary. I've never been one for therapy, and there's nothing wrong with me—I just let my anger get the best of me. Jake knows how to push my buttons."

"First of all, Carl, coaching is not therapy—it's coaching. It allows you to explore what motivates you and what 'pushes your buttons,' as you mention. It can help you make sense of your problems and design a solid plan to cope with myriad stressors and work issues that make you feel stuck."

Carl was stunned and had an intense feeling of uneasiness. Why would Ines think he needed a coach? This was making him feel very awkward. "Once again, I truly apologize for to-day—but I really don't think this is necessary. Honestly, Jake and I can try to work this out between us. I'll eat the humble pie, even though it's his fault."

"There's more here to deal with than this one instance." Ines went on, "Try to keep an open mind." Carl started to speak, but Ines stopped him. "At this particular juncture I'm going to have to insist you do this. I just don't see how we can move forward in a positive direction if you don't."

Carl bristled in his chair.

"Stay positive." Ines spoke softly and reassuringly. "You might actually learn something, and it certainly can't hurt."

*Wow…how could it get to this point? My boss is telling me I have no choice but to get help. She must think I'm pretty far gone…*

Carl couldn't stop thinking about what had happened, for the remainder of the day.

*It's not even my fault, and Ines is asking me to see a coach.*

All he could do was go through the motions until 5:00 p.m., when he jumped back in his car to drive home. As he pulled out of the parking lot, another thought hit him. *What the heck am I going to tell Maria? I wonder if I should even tell her…she might just use it against me.*

◆

Carl felt his heart pumping as he jockeyed through the lanes of traffic—he had to get to home. He needed to have a drink and sort out what had happened. He also wondered how he would broach the subject with Maria. There was no way he could go through the process of seeing a coach unless he had that conversation with his wife, he realized.

*Why do I need to do this when there are so many people at Solar who are useless?! We need a serious talent overhaul across the company! Why doesn't Ines realize that? And what about Jake? Shouldn't he be the one who needs coaching?*

Carl was fuming, once again. He turned on the radio, which was playing one of his favorite folk songs from days gone by. The lilting voice of the singer helped to calm him somewhat. He turned up the radio and focused on the song, trying to put the day, and his ordeals, behind him.

*Some days are heavy as the night*
*Inky shadows breaking through the light*
*It never rains, it pours,*
*Little by little*
*For time slips through our fingers*
*The ghosts that ever linger*
*They whisper in the wind*

*Trouble never leaves you,*
*From this you may not flee*
*So when the dark of night seems boundless*
*Just remember me...just remember me.*

# CHAPTER THREE

MARIA SAT ON THE COUCH and reread the text from Carl. His message had been vague and, therefore, nerve-wracking. She read it over again. Something about how they "need to talk." Maria had left early that Friday, canceling her afternoon appointments at the bank. She'd decided to come home and start dinner for the two of them since Sam was out at a movie with his two cousins for the evening. She had also been trying to subdue a slightly sick feeling in the pit of her stomach, as she feared there might be an impending implication of "doom" that framed the text.

*Dear God, don't let him be fired.*

◆

Maria had stopped to buy seafood and fresh vegetables on the way home, including the beautifully crisp green asparagus reminding her that spring was around the corner even if it was a steely gray pallor outside her kitchen window.

Maria knew they would have to have a talk—and a long one. She hoped they could have a discussion about a reexamination of their relationship. Carl was so harsh with her these days. He was so deep into his issues at work; he barely looked up from his phone or laptop when he came home, apart from when he was tuning out in front of the TV.

Maria walked into the dining room and lit the candles under the glass hurricane. "How long has it been since we lit candles in the house?" she wondered aloud. The candles left a warm glow in the dining room, softening the edges of everything. No sharp corners, no sharp words…that was what she wished for. She longed for things to be different.

The fatigue from far too many nights of insomnia due to her near-constant worry about Carl's increasing anger and frustration was really getting to Maria. And then there was her son's detachment. Sam barely spoke to his parents these days. He seemed so distant, almost completely unwilling to communicate, and she realized he was spending far too much time on his phone.

◆

Maria heard the key in the lock. The thump of Carl's brief-case and the huge sigh he released as he crossed the threshold were all she needed to take the temperature of his mood. But Maria was determined to make this a relaxing—and hopefully progressive—evening. She had to figure out what was going on.

She went to greet Carl. "How was your day, hon?"

"Ugh…oh man, I need a drink," he answered.

"I made a nice fish dinner and even got us a few shrimps for an appetizer," Maria offered, extending her hand. "Come sit down and relax in the living room with me."

*Boy, she's really trying tonight… How do I broach the subject?*

"Mmm nice…I can smell it. Can't we just move to Spain and become fish mongers?" Carl joked. She let out a quiet "ohhhh, if only…!" recalling their trip there, the year after they first met. He remembered with a sense of wistfulness when he'd accompanied Maria to her native country. She had taken him fishing in the Mediterranean. It was like nothing he had ever experienced: salt, sand and earth, mixed with the faint scent of the freshest seafood known to man. He remembered the little seaport near her family home, where boat fishing in the shoals was particularly good for catching red snapper and channel mackerel. The way the sun shone on her hair and in

◆

her eyes when they were on the water, and the heady scent of the salty, sun-dappled seawater, was intoxicating. He remembered the laughter too, and how she had teased him about being the "American pirate" of their little rowboat.

"Seriously, I'd love to just throw in the towel."

Maria began to get fidgety. "Why do you say that, Carl? You used to have such excitement for your position—and all the inspiring and creative new projects."

"Well," Carl began, "things got pretty heated at the office today—with Jake. Afterward, Ines spoke to both of us in her office. When all was said and done, Ines took me aside and let me know that she thinks I need to see a coach. God knows why she doesn't think Jake should be the one to get help—she thinks it's all me!" Carl rolled his eyes and then stood up to go into the kitchen. Maria spoke to him from the living room.

"Actually, Carl, looking at it from another perspective, that might be a good thing. It might help you figure out why you have so much anger and resentment bottled up inside and why you feel so strongly about what happened with the job in Dubai."

Carl was rattling around in the drawers in the kitchen. "Where the heck is the corkscrew?"

Maria came to help, handing him the corkscrew, two glasses and the chilled bottle of wine from the refrigerator. "I know it's been a tough go with all the technical issues and prob-lems you've encountered," she began, "but things have really changed for you. I feel like your nerves are on fire these days. Any little incident seems to set you off."

Carl popped the cork on the bottle, pouring generously into the wine glass, and gulped down almost half a glass before beginning to speak. "Maria, do you think it's easy doing the job I do? With all I have to deal with?"

"Well, no, of course I don't. It's just that…"

"It's just that you think you know what I go through, or how I should react, or basically how to live my life!" Carl's face flushed. "Do you know how hard it was for someone like me to even get a good job like that?"

"That's what I'm referring to, Carl. I'm really worried about you," Maria said earnestly. "You don't seem to be able to dis-cuss anything without blowing up. It's a little scary." She moved toward him and began to rub his shoulders to try to calm him down. Maria was concerned about Carl's health and noticed he drank too much too quickly and became flushed when he drank as well as when his mood became inflamed—which hap-pened far too often. Carl pulled away and went back to the liv-ing room couch.

"Please, Carl, let's talk about this."

He looked up from his wine glass. "Maria, I think I could be in serious trouble."

Maria offered him the poached shrimp with cocktail sauce and almost dropped the tray. "What do you mean?"

He turned to face his wife. "You need to know something, Maria. You need to know that because of Jake's ineptitude and all the problems with the Dubai job—the delays, the dichroic film deteriorating during transport...and everything else..." He paused, then let out a whoosh of air before continuing. "Because of all that, I'm not going to get my bonus this year. Which means that all the money we owe on the credit card right now and all the other bills that need to be paid—it will all have to wait. It's going to really hurt us, and we're going to get dinged with interest. And now, on top of it all, Ines is mandating me to 'get help.' I really don't understand it."

*There. I said it. Now I just have to put up with Maria's exhaustive way of trying to understand issues from every possible angle.*

Maria sighed. That was, indeed, a blow to them financially. Why hadn't he told her before this? No wonder he had refused to go out to eat and kept changing the subject about getting new windows. But Maria knew that this was not the time to ask those questions; it would just incense him, and they'd never get

◆

anywhere.

*No, just stay the course with your mandate for the evening to get Carl to talk about what on earth is going on with him. And to talk about what's going on with Sam.*

"Well, I guess we just have to budget for it, Carl. Maybe the next six months will be different. We aren't going to starve; we just have to be more careful." She paused for a beat before continuing. "But back to the coach idea. I'm curious, how does Ines feel about the Dubai job? Does *she* feel it was all Jake's fault or does she think other issues may have contributed to its failure?" Maria knew she was treading on thin ice and was circumspect in her delivery. "Again, maybe working with a coach will help you figure out some things and how they went wrong for you, without shame or blame. You might be able to work more effectively—and hopefully more amenably—with Jake. He's not going anywhere, right? And neither are you."

"I wish he would go—right out the door. I don't know, Maria. I feel like everything happened so fast with that job, and it went south before I even realized what was transpiring. Sometimes I feel like everything is happening at high speed."

"I know, so do I," Maria offered, "particularly with Sam."

"What do you mean?"

"Haven't you noticed how withdrawn he's become lately?

He barely speaks to us anymore."

"He's completely shut *me* out," Carl said in agreement. "Whenever I ask him how school is he just shrugs and says, 'OK' before going back to his phone. He used to be so engaged with both of us. Do you think it's a phase?"

"No, I'm concerned. I don't think it's a phase. I don't know what happened to his friends from the neighborhood—they never come around anymore. He's withdrawn and seems so sullen. I just hope he's not depressed or experiencing something more serious. I was thinking I should contact the school to see if they've noticed anything that might be affecting him. We can't just ignore it."

"More serious—what do you mean?" Carl got edgy at the thought of what he assumed his wife could be implying.

"I don't know…what if it's drugs?" I mean, he's so young, but you never know these days."

"You're right, Maria. Whatever you want to do is fine by me. I can't get two words out of him."

"Come on, Carl, come into the kitchen and help me with the rest of the dinner."

◆

It was nearly impossible to find parking in the lot of Café au Lait. Carl sat with the engine running for almost ten minutes before someone left and he was able to pull into a spot. Good thing he'd arrived early.

He still wasn't sure about meeting Joe. Over the years, Joe had been like a second father to him. Joe had always been there for Carl, through all the junctures in his life—the good times and not so good. He was a rock for Carl. He felt bad about the fact that he and Joe hadn't stayed in touch much during the past few years—not since Carl had become estranged from his dad. It made him feel a little uncomfortable, considering Joe was a friend to them both, and Carl worried that Joe would be judgmental of him for deciding to distance himself from his father in recent years.

The café was humming on Saturday morning, full of college students, young moms and friends meeting for coffee on one of their treasured days off.

Maria had initiated the call to Joe the night before, while they were preparing the final elements of dinner. She'd suggested that Carl should take the opportunity to talk about work, Sam, and his issues with his father with someone who knew them both and could offer another perspective as to how Carl and his dad might "bury the hatchet." She'd insisted he give Joe a call right then and there, as she'd known he would put it off if he didn't do it immediately. The pre-dinner wine had been making him a little more receptive to the idea, and she'd known he might soften to her suggestion.

Carl had called Joe on his cell phone from the kitchen, and he had picked up right away. Carl had asked if they could meet "sometime in the near future" and had been surprised to hear Joe say, "No time like the present, Carl—how about tomorrow?"

Joe was sitting at a table by the window. Carl chuckled to himself. *He must be the only human in this place with no cell phone, iPad, laptop or other device. He just sits there looking out the window...or gazing around the room. He looks like a bit of an oddball.*

Joe got up to give Carl a hug as he walked over to the table. "It's been far too long, Carl."

"I agree, Joe. Thanks for taking the time to meet. I'm going to grab something—I'll be right back. Do you want anything?"

"I'm good, still have this one." Joe gestured toward a steaming cup.

*What am I going to say to him? I hope he doesn't start lecturing me.*

Carl sat down with his cappuccino and shrugged off his coat onto the chair. "Thanks again for getting together on such short notice."

"Well, a retiree tends to have a little more time on their

hands," he said, smiling warmly. "Besides, I really wanted to see how you were doing, Carl. How are Maria and Sam?"

"They're OK, although Sam is definitely going through what I call EAR. That's short for early adolescent reticence."

Joe chuckled. "A little withdrawn, is he? As long as he still talks to you both, I'm sure he's OK. It's pretty typical—though, I'll admit, it's somewhat early for that. Have you or Maria been able to break the silence with him?"

"Not really, Joe. We are getting a bit concerned, but Maria has a plan to find out what's going on—and hopefully we can figure out how to bring him out of his shell."

"That's a good thing. What about you? How's work, Carl?"

"Not great these days. I had a major project go south—the company lost a lot of money, and I lost my bonus—not exactly the highlight of my career."

Carl took a sip of his coffee. Joe remained silent, holding Carl's gaze as if waiting for him to say something further. Carl stiffened slightly in his chair. That was the thing about Joe; there were times when it felt like he could look right through you.

After early retirement, Joe had spent some time in Asia and had taken to exploring the art and science of meditation. He had been an annual visitor to a ten-day silent-meditation re-treat in Chaiya, southern Thailand, for eight years in a row. Joe described it as "a spiritual paradise," with open-air meditation halls and spectacular manicured forests surrounding a monastery. It had become both an idyllic refuge from his stormy life after a twenty-year career as an executive for a derivatives trading firm and the perfect place to deepen his practice. Conditions were decidedly rugged, and the mosquitoes were the size of dragonflies, but he always returned renewed and brimming with further insight and inner peace.

"What else?" Joe asked, calmly.

"Well…my boss wants me to meet with a coach. That just infuriates me."

Joe looked up at Carl and smiled. "Change is never easy—but it's definitely better than the alternative."

Carl chuckled. "Yes, you're right. And I guess it's never too late to learn."

"Right, Carl. So if you accept that as truth, then you have to unlock your mind—and stay open to the possibilities."

"What sort of possibilities? I don't think I need a coach—what I need is for my coworker to clean up his act."

Joe's silence was palpable. Carl took a breath and then spoke more thoughtfully. "I suppose I have to look at it more positively though, since I know it's unavoidable."

"So what do you want to accomplish with the coach?"

◆

"Accomplish…? Not sure I understand, Joe."

"Maybe you should do some self-reflection on this—maybe journal about your goals for this coaching engagement. Honestly, I think of it as an open window."

"An open window…?"

"Yes, when you get home, once you've had a chance to journal your thoughts and goals about this new opportunity, take the time to do a brief visualization."

"OK…what do I visualize?"

"Well, you close your eyes and imagine a beautiful scene… it can be anywhere that brings you the utmost peace. And then zero in on an open window—a panorama of the most spectacular view you've ever seen… The window can be wherever you imagine—a home, a castle, whatever brings you feelings of harmony and joy. And by looking through that window, you see your future—more clearly and brilliantly, and much more positively, than you do in this moment. Imagine every detail, right down to the colors, scents and sounds of every part of that future image emerging on the other side. And within that picture, envision your future self—wiser, more positive, and free from anger and resentment—after working with your new teacher."

Carl felt a little awkward in these moments. Here he was in the middle of a coffee shop, closing his eyes slightly, listening to the sound of Joe's voice.

"It's OK, Carl, you can practice at home." Joe smiled.

"Right, I know. Got carried away for a second. OK, I'll do my best with all of this. So I'm guessing you think this is a good thing that I am meeting with a coach?"

"Of course! And, you're committed to doing everything you need to do to realize a positive outcome, correct?"

"Well...yes."

"Then you must honor your obligations with others and commit to the learning. It's a wonderful opportunity and a blessing to gain perspective in life. Embrace it!"

Joe always had a way of drilling down to the most significant truth of any situation. It was his gift.

Carl went on to further explain to Joe what had happened at work, his struggles dealing with others' expectations, his inability to control himself and his diminishing health. He expressed his worries about finances, his deep concerns regarding Sam, the confrontation with Jake and general feelings of being lost at sea.

The two men talked for what seemed like a short time, but when Carl looked at his watch he realized it had been almost two hours. He looked out the window and saw a glowing red orb between the trees—the sun was setting in the wintery sky.

"Guess I'd better head back, Joe. I promised Maria I'd pick up pizza tonight. I can't thank you enough for today. It's helped me a lot, just talking it through."

"Keep in touch, Carl. Let's do this again, say, in a few weeks? I'm really looking forward to learning more about your sessions with the coach. It's going to be a very enlightening experience for you—I'm certain of it."

Carl felt relieved and more at peace than he had been in a very long time. He wished he could hold on to that feeling forever.

◆

When Carl got home that night and Maria was upstairs in the shower, he went into his study and pulled out the notebook from the desk drawer. He felt compelled to write his feelings...

*It's strange, I almost feel hopeful again,* he wrote. *Maybe Joe and Maria are right. It seems like this coaching engagement is an opportunity to learn. Things have been so crazy for me lately. I just want to understand why I react the way I do. It's overwhelming some days. I'm worried about my marriage and my son, and work has become such an overpowering, heavy burden. I need that load to lighten.*

# CHAPTER FOUR

THE ANTIQUE CLOCK TICKED LOUDLY. It seemed odd amid the soothing blue-green walls and watery landscape prints. Carl was in the waiting room of his new coach's office. He felt nervous and yet filled with a sense of optimism that he had not expected.

*It must have been my talk with Joe.*

Ines had sent the coach's bio in advance, and though she seemed qualified enough, Carl still felt a sense of trepidation regarding a coaching engagement. But he was also curious and decided to try to remain positive. As Joe so wisely put it, his company was investing in his career development, not setting

◆

him up to get him fired. Yet he still wondered how he could be forthright with a coach. After all, the company was footing the bill—so where would the coach's loyalty lie? And what about confidentiality?

The door to the waiting room opened and a distinguished-looking woman strode across the room and shook Carl's hand firmly.

"Hi, Carl, it is a pleasure to meet you. I'm Flora. How are you?"

"Flora…as in 'flower'? That's an Italian name, right? Yet I detect a very slight Scottish brogue."

"Yes, on both accounts." Flora smiled. "My father was Italian—it was his mother's name. He married a Scottish woman, and that's where I grew up—in the 'Land of the Gaels'—until we came here when I was twelve. My accent is *almost* gone though." She grinned.

Carl could feel his mouth drying out. He was more nervous now that all this buildup was, in fact, a reality.

Flora motioned him into her office. It was as soothing and warm as the waiting room. "Come in and take a seat, Carl." She gestured toward a comfortable-looking two-seat sofa with several colorful pillows. "I can appreciate that working with a coach might be a bit unsettling. Let's talk about how you are

♦

feeling about all of this."

"OK. I guess I'm just not sure *how* I feel about it."

"I am sure your first reaction was to jump for joy when you heard that we would be working together." Flora smiled.

"Well, you could say that." Carl laughed nervously.

"I can appreciate that. So tell me, jokes aside, what is your understanding of the purpose behind us working together?"

"My boss, Ines, said that it's due to my performance—my sales numbers are down and I'm not currently meeting projections. Plus, she may have mentioned the fact that I had a bit of a blowup at work with a coworker, so she wanted to get me some help."

"Yes, that is my understanding as well. So let me just say right off the top that my role as your coach is to support *you*. I can help you identify your strengths and show you how to leverage them—as well as identify your development opportunities. How does that sound to you?"

Carl exhaled and laughed nervously. "Well, that sounds pretty good. So you're not going to be too hard on me then, are you?"

Flora laughed, "I will do my best not to. I don't believe anyone jumps out of bed in the morning with the intention to disappoint, even if their behavior does disappoint others. To put it simply, I believe that most people are doing the best that they can, and that they just haven't found a better way yet. What do *you* think of that?"

"I would definitely agree with that." Carl paused and took a breath before continuing. "I must say things are really not working for me, both at home and at work."

"Well, I would love to help you. And, before we go any further, please know that what you share with me is confidential."

Flora could see the look of relief in Carl's eyes. "I spoke with Ines this morning and asked her what her goals and expectations were for our work together—and I will share that with you—but she understands and agrees that our conversations shall remain confidential. She just wants you to get the help and support that you need."

"Well, that's good to know. I was wondering about the confidentiality aspect for sure—and, of course, I want to hear more about her expectations of our sessions."

"OK, we can discuss that. But first, I want to focus on you. You mentioned that things are not working right now at home and work. Why don't we start first with what's going on at home?"

Carl began by mentioning the worry he had over the lack of communication with his son and how he and his wife didn't seem to be on the same page. He began hesitantly, but once he started, the thoughts poured out. It actually felt good talking to someone instead of keeping everything inside.

"Thanks, Carl. This is very helpful. So tell me…how would you *like* the relationship between you and your wife to be? In other words, can you describe what the ideal husband and wife relationship would look like to you?"

"OK…well, to start, it would be nice if we could have a conversation that doesn't lead to an argument. She claims I never listen to her."

"Is that true?"

"Maybe sometimes…but I don't mean to *not* listen. I just get so frustrated, and I feel so much pressure to do the right thing. It seems like no matter what I do or say, I've blown it with her. I don't know what to do to make her happy anymore. I find myself shutting down and tuning her out."

"It's OK, Carl, we can work through this. And your son, Sam, what is not working with him?"

"Well he's thirteen—in the throes of the 'terrible teens'— and it seems like I can't get through to him anymore. If I ask him how his day was, he just says, 'fine' and walks away. I can't seem to even get a conversation going with him these days. He either shuts down or ignores me."

"Well, I can see why that would be frustrating. We will address this as well. So we've talked a bit about what's happening at home. What about work?"

"I've had some great years there…but lately it's been one thing after another. Budget issues, project delays and things getting way out of hand on overages because of late deliveries and technical issues. Then there are the problems I have with other departments, like Production. The manager of that division and I are always at odds—which is what led to the final crescendo." Carl laughed.

"What do you mean? Do you find yourself getting frustrated or angry more easily?"

"I hate to admit this, but yes, and it is not helping me in my situation at work or at home."

Flora began slowly, "It sounds like a core issue here is that when you find yourself dealing with a difficult conversation or problem, you might not have the emotional composure or resilience to see it through. Does that sound accurate?"

"Yes, it does, actually. It's strange, I don't remember having such a short fuse before. But certainly over the last year, I seem to have very little patience—for anything, really."

"Why do you think that is?"

"I have been under so much pressure. There's a term in

♦

football called 'piling on.' "

"What do you mean, Carl? You'll have to forgive me, sorry, not a big follower of the sport."

"It's a phrase that describes the action of players jumping on top of a player after a tackle has been made. Well, quite honestly, I feel like the guy at the bottom of that pile. And on top of my issues at home and at work, I'm also in debt up to my eyeballs. I was counting on a bonus that never came through because of all the missed budget projections and corresponding late penalties from clients on projects that went south. I guess that's why I'm a little hot-tempered."

"It sounds like you've had your fair share of challenges, that's for certain. Would it be helpful if I showed you some ways that you can build emotional composure so that when you find yourself in a high-stakes or emotionally charged conversation, you will be able to stay focused, fully present and able to navigate the discussion more easily?"

Carl looked dubious. "You can do that?"

"Yes, definitely."

Carl laughed. "Well, heck yeah! But I have to say that I am a bit skeptical. Sounds too good to be true...no offense."

Flora laughed. "None taken. I'm not going to lie to you; it may not necessarily be easy—but it's doable for sure. It takes some practice and a little time to build good habits and skills. Basically, we will be addressing two primary areas. You might like the names, due to your affinity for sports. The first one I call the 'inside game,' which refers to the habits, traits, beliefs and personal tendencies that make each of us unique. In particular, we each experience the world around us, and within us, differently. Unfortunately, we often assume others sense and perceive the world just like we do, but of course, this isn't the case. As a result, these natural differences can create a lot of misunderstandings, misalignment and conflict. And then there is conflict avoidance, which, by the way, is just as destructive."

This was really getting interesting. People's differing beliefs and viewpoints causing conflict…Carl had never thought of it that way. He could really feel himself getting tuned in to what Flora was saying.

"Throughout our life, each of us has developed unique ways of responding to and coping with our environment, and not all of our tactics are effective. For example, when feeling strong negative emotions, one person might respond with anger whereas another might respond by withdrawing."

"I hear you. I have a tendency to withdraw when I am angry, and Maria wants to talk everything out."

"Great observation. You now know firsthand that how one

person handles negative emotion can be so dissimilar from another. This causes a great deal of confusion. For example, Maria may have a hard time understanding why you won't open up to her. She may wonder how you will ever solve anything if you don't talk about it. My guess is you withdraw for fear of not saying or doing the right thing and making things worse. And when you have spoken up in the past, your anger was evident and that bothered her."

"That's exactly right! You hit the nail on the head. Why can't she see this?"

"Again, it goes back to the fact that each person has their own coping mechanisms and strategies, and the key is to get out of judgment about that and come to understand. Only then can you begin to solve anything. We solve nothing when we are in a state of judgment. We just make things worse."

"That's really true… So the burning question is, how do I get out of this mess?"

"This is exactly what we will be working on, among other things."

Carl moved forward on the sofa. Flora could see that reviewing the process was intriguing Carl. "Could you be a bit more specific?" he asked.

"Sure. So I talked about the inside game. The other side

of the equation is the 'outside game,' which consists of a set of skills and techniques that help you navigate a conversation, from beginning to end, for the purpose of what I refer to as 'achieving meaningful alignment.' These skills can be taught, but to successfully apply them, it is vital for us to understand why we tend to interact and respond to others the way that we do—that's the 'inside game' part. The two parts work hand in hand."

"OK...that makes sense."

"Now, you mentioned that you and Jake are, shall we say, not aligned or on the same page, correct?"

Carl chuckled. "Well, that's an understatement."

"The skills that I have mentioned will all assist you to have a productive conversation with Jake so that you can gain alignment on how your current and future projects need to get resolved. These skills will be useful for when you want to gain alignment with anyone, on any topic, so this will also help you with Sam and Maria as well."

"Well, if you can do that, I'm in!"

"That's great, Carl. Why don't I walk you through my coaching process, timeframe, and goals to be reached...that sort of thing. Sound good?"

"Absolutely."

Flora explained more about the coaching engagement and what to expect once they concluded their time together.

"I am excited to work with you, Carl. The ability to regulate your emotions is very important, as you know, both at home and at work. You are certainly not alone; many, if not most, of us are challenged to keep emotionally composed during important personal and professional conversations. Many feel ill-equipped to have meaningful conversations because we lack the competence, confidence and comfort to do so. Often, the outcome is avoiding the conversation all together or jumping in and bulldozing our way through. I think you can agree that neither approach will yield a good outcome."

"That's for sure." Carl looked off and said thoughtfully, "I also know that I need to sit down with Maria and clear the air… At least last time we talked we were civil to one another."

"Well, that's good to hear. Tell me more."

"It was just like you said. I was reluctant to tell Maria that I was not going to get the bonus we both had come to expect, and that Ines wanted me to work with a coach. I knew I had to tell her, but I was afraid to do it. As you mentioned, I avoided talking with her about things because I wasn't sure how she was going to react and then how I would handle that. I knew that I seem to be short-tempered lately, so I honestly wasn't sure how

I would react to her. You know, to her credit, she was pretty cool about it."

"I'm glad the conversation went well."

"It was good to get it out on the table. We even had a nice discussion regarding Sam and his behavior of late. Luckily, we agree that something is not right with him, and we are both concerned. He just buries his head in his phone all the time."

Flora nodded in agreement. "This brings up an important point, Carl. Many of us are feeling increased pressure due to advances in technology. Although we *can* be available 24/7 because of our phones, computers and other devices, that doesn't mean that we *should* be available. Many of us have fallen into the habit of relying too heavily on technology. This has increased stress for most of us. We seem to have lost the art of human connection and the ability to have conversations—important conversations both at work and at home that we *need* to have."

Carl was really engrossed in the discussion. It seemed to him that most people just didn't talk to each other anymore. They had "shut down" in terms of just having a dialogue about any subject. Emails and texts always trumped phone calls and in-person meetings.

"Wow…that's really true. It is so difficult just to sit down and have a conversation with someone. Everyone seems so rushed. Also, if I go to a two-hour meeting I know that by the end I will have fifty more emails. I feel the pressure to check them while I'm in the meeting, and therefore, I haven't really been listening and engaged. It is not just me doing this, by the way; I see this with everyone. It's counterproductive and, frankly, wastes everyone's time, but that seems to be the way it goes these days. You know, it's become an acceptable business practice."

"Yes. I can understand how this habit gets formed and how pulled we can feel to check the phone. Who wants to have fifty emails to tackle at the end of the meeting? Yet, as you said, it really doesn't work. We can discuss some ways to stay engaged in a meeting and manage the technology better."

"Sounds great. In fact, I'm actually looking forward to this coaching thing."

"Me too. I know that I can help you." Flora wrote down her email address on a card and then handed it to Carl. "One thing I would like to do is have you complete an assessment. This particular assessment is designed to help you identify how you are more likely to respond in a high-stakes, high-impact, and often emotionally charged, type of conversation—just like the ones that you have been describing at home and work. This allows us to tap into that inside game part I spoke about earlier.

The results will give us a great data point to discuss. Then, based on your results, we'll create a plan to help you work on areas of opportunity for growth. Sound good?"

"Sure, I took an assessment before, but it was a long time ago. Sounds interesting."

"It is. I'm going to send you the link to complete it, and in our next session I'll review your results with you."

"OK, sounds good."

Flora got up and shook Carl's hand. "Thanks for talking with me today. I'm eager for you to discover all the ways that you can build emotional composure and resilience—and how to navigate through these tough conversations with more ease and comfort. We both know that you and Jake need to get aligned pretty quickly—as well as you, Maria and Sam. Do you agree?"

"Absolutely, Flora."

"OK, let's meet next week. Please email me some date and time options."

"Will do. Thanks again."

Carl walked out to the parking lot and took a deep breath. He looked around. Somehow, everything—the sky…the trees… even the cars in the parking lot—looked a little brighter. He felt a sense of enthusiasm along with anticipation. It was the most unfamiliar, extraordinary sensation, but he welcomed it with open arms.

# CHAPTER FIVE

EARLY SPRING WAS PARTICULARLY GRAY and barren, especially driving along this stretch of the river, where the frozen trees bent forward, yielding to the weight of their branches heavy-laden with ice. It always made Carl more thoughtful as he made his way into town along the river—and sometimes just a little downhearted. Summer on the riverfront was so full of life—such a stark contrast to the scene that wound ahead of him. This time, however, the drive didn't feel so desolate. It just felt...neutral.

Carl's thoughts were his constant companion of late, and today was no different. All of these emotional explosions, the hostility, suspicion and anger…it had become so exhausting being…*him*. He had revisited some of his notebook entries the night before and realized how withdrawn he had become, as well, avoiding social encounters and get-togethers.

But Carl was beginning to feel a little differently. He had hope. And he trusted in this new process—it just made sense. The results of the online assessment seemed to make sense too. Even though he didn't quite understand what the results meant, he already had an idea they were pretty accurate. He scored high in an approach referred to as "Directive" and low in a "Harmonious" style.

Carl smiled, thinking about it. *High directive; low harmonious… Yes, that pretty much sums things up. You might say I am far too direct with pretty much everyone…and, no, there isn't much harmony in my life at the moment!*

Still, he felt good about doing something to change his situation, and he was looking forward to his follow-up appointment with Flora. This new opportunity seemed to give him a sense of purpose.

*All good…*

As he walked into Flora's waiting area, she opened her office door.

"Perfect timing! Come on in. How have you been, Carl?"

◆

"Pretty good actually, Flora. A bit better than last week."

"Well, that's good to hear." Flora smiled. "Tell me more."

Carl settled into the sofa and leaned forward. "You know, I've done a lot of thinking since we talked last time. I even wrote a bit in my notebook."

"Your notebook? What is that?"

"A while back, I felt that I needed to jot down some thoughts, and so I have this notebook that I write in. It kind of helps me to get things out of my head and onto paper. Sort of like venting—but by way of writing instead of talking things through with someone."

"I see… I think that is a great idea, and I would encourage you to continue this practice. So you said you have been doing some thinking. What about?"

"About this whole situation. Like how did I get myself into this nightmare with Jake? As well, I've been trying to figure out why I have so many challenges at home with Maria and Sam. I realize that I need to take some personal responsibility for the decisions I made that led up to all of this."

Carl paused and looked out the window, then he continued. "Regarding Jake and the project, I still believe he is just as much to blame as I am—but I could have handled it better, that's for certain."

Flora nodded in agreement. "Recognizing that there might be a better way to handle the project issue with Jake is keen insight on your part, Carl. As I've mentioned, I feel we often have good intentions but simply don't know how to do things differently to achieve positive results."

"Right. I'm really interested to know your feedback on my assessment."

"Yes, I see that you completed it. Thank you for that."

"I found the questions interesting and—maybe I'm jumping ahead here—I wondered if it might even be a good idea to have Maria and Sam take it. It is just a thought. I ran it by Maria and she thought it was a great plan. Actually, asking her to take it seemed to put her in a good mood." Carl smiled. "I guess she was encouraged by that. She even suggested that the three of us go out to dinner as a family—at an inexpensive restaurant, of course." He chuckled. "Unfortunately, Sam declined, opting to have a friend over and order a pizza. He said they needed to do their homework together, but I'm sure there were some video games involved," he said, smiling wryly.

"So how did you both feel about that?"

"Maria and I were disappointed that he didn't want to come, but we didn't let it spoil the moment for us."

"I think it is a great idea for Maria and Sam to take the

◆

assessment as well. And I am glad that Sam's response did not dampen your and Maria's spirits too much. Sam will come around. I know it is hard for you to see that he is behaving this way."

"Yes, it really is."

"One step at a time. Let's review your results."

"OK good, let's go."

"You will see that this assessment has six styles represented: Diligent, Interdependent, Harmonious, Cautious, Directive, and Courageous. Remember, the context here is how you are *most likely* to respond in conversations that have high stakes or a high impact. In other words, in a discussion in which it is important for you to gain alignment with another," Flora explained. "You scored highest in Directive and lowest in Harmonious. I am just going to hit the highlights for you here, as there is much more for you to read in the report, but basically behavior depicting High Directive is what I would describe as bold and competitive. Of course many of us use this approach when we give orders, make our demands known and provide directions to others. If a Directive approach is balanced, we are assertive, and our thoughts and approach to a discussion are very clear. However, the more intense these feelings are, the less likely it is that the feeling or approach will be constructive.

◆

The competitive feelings and the desire to win can overshadow the more positive aspects of clarity and confidence in our knowledge and experience."

"So I guess it's about things going 'my way or the highway.'" Carl grinned.

"Yes, you could say that. But it's also about control. And even your sense of security."

"That's interesting."

"It's as if the underlying message is 'I have to be sure I'm not going to be taken advantage of.' Or it can show up in meetings as, 'If I don't voice my opinion—loudly—someone is going to undermine my view.' "

"Hmmm…if you are on the receiving end, I guess it can seem pretty obnoxious."

"Well, it can if it's not tempered properly, yes. I mentioned security as well. There's an aspect of this approach that relates to self-promotion and self-protection. So if you are feeling threatened—either by the circumstances or by the person in front of you—a High Directive approach can derail the conversation."

"So…I'm ripping the Band-Aid off too quickly. I'm too blunt."

"In certain situations, yes. What do you think?"

"I think you're right…"

"The other consideration is body language. When we adopt a Directive approach with intense passion, our body language can *force* others into compliance or disengagement."

"So they disengage just to make me stop barking orders, right?"

Flora nodded and continued. "Well, yes, but that doesn't mean that they've bought into what you were saying or that you've gained their commitment. So you're far from settling the issue. Does this feel right to you?"

"Yes, absolutely. I can see how this happens—not only at work but at home as well."

"Can you give me an example of when High Directive might have shown up either at work or home?"

"Well, the most obvious one is how I handled the situation with Jake."

"Great observation. Flora sat back in her chair and paused before continuing. "You know, it might be helpful to write down your thoughts on this further when you have some downtime."

"Yes, absolutely."

"OK, let's move on," Flora looked down at her notes.

"You scored lowest in Harmonious. The Harmonious approach refers to accommodating the needs of others. It can be a positive approach when based on selflessness, admiration and trust. People who score highest in this category are very conscientious—real team players. So Harmonious dialogue is focused on pleasing the other person and smoothing over the tension."

"Well, I can see why I scored low in that category!"

"OK. Why do you say that?"

"Well, it just makes sense. I'm never concerned about someone else's feelings when I am trying to get my point across and I know that is it really important... I guess I thought I was being assertive, but really, it could be that I am too aggressive. I can see why my current approach doesn't always work."

"Great job, Carl. You're already owning how your natural tendencies to gain alignment with people may not always be the most effective approach, particularly when you feel very strongly about something."

"So how do I fix this?"

"I appreciate your enthusiasm. We will work through this together, step by step."

"This profile report has really been insightful for me, Flora. And the accuracy of the results makes me want to ask Maria and Sam to take this. It would be interesting to see how they score. It might also be a good bridge for Jake and me. Maybe this would be a way that the two of us could start to move forward together."

"Both are excellent thoughts. It is a good first step for sure, for all concerned. As I mentioned before, only when we can get out of judgment and blame—and have the *willingness* to understand why someone is doing what they are doing—can we hope to solve anything. Not always an easy thing to do, I might add."

"That's for sure! You just want to blast the other person, as I did with Jake."

"Here is a little homework for you." Flora smiled. "Between now and our next session, observe how the Directive style comes into play, and if you would, please write these observations in your notebook so we can discuss them next time."

Flora hesitated for a moment then asked, "How are you feeling about all of this, Carl?"

"Actually, I am encouraged. This assessment explained so much, and now I just want to be sure that I fix things. I don't want to go on wondering when I'm going to step on the next land mine!"

"No, that's no way to live—I wholeheartedly agree." Flora laughed.

◆

Carl had a slight spring in his step as he left Flora's office. It felt like he could finally see the other side of obscurity. A light

◆

through the shadows of who he *could* be instead of who he had been…beyond the knee-jerk reactions and relentless frustration. It was a sense of calm in knowing that he might be able to get a glimpse of what was on the other side of his anger and his misplaced emotional responses. Most of all, he loved the fact that he had the chance to explore his life like this. It was like having a bird's-eye view—almost like a secret that no one else possessed—that he was able to observe and learn from.

Most of all, Carl felt a sense of gratitude that he had a *choice*. A choice to move out of the all-encompassing exasperation he had been experiencing—and with Flora's help, the choice to make things better.

# CHAPTER SIX

CARL COULDN'T REMEMBER THE LAST TIME he'd had such a nice dinner with his family. That night, Maria had prepared vegetarian fare—which usually did not excite Carl in the least. To his utter surprise, it turned out to be incredibly delicious. Stuffed acorn squash with quinoa, chickpeas and other veggies, spiked with goat cheese—and toasted pine nuts sprinkled on top.

"I can't believe how amazing this is," Carl remarked. "It almost tastes meaty, somehow."

"See? You can still make great meals with no meat," Maria said, smiling.

Sam grumbled about the food and barely ate the squash,

but he ate all the quinoa stuffing.

"How do you like it, Sam?"

"It's sort of all right, Mom…I guess," was all he could manage.

It was the conversation at the dinner table that was much more animated than usual. Carl was still on a high after his session with Flora and discussed taking the assessments as a family, suggesting that it might help improve their communication at home. He was buoyant in his explanation of the process.

"Hey, Sam, do you remember that movie I rented for you when you were a kid, *Teenage Mutant Ninja Turtles*?"

"Yeah, uh…lame! What about it, Dad?"

"Oh, come on, remember you loved that character, the huge mouse…what was his name?"

"Splinter? He was a rat, actually. What about him?"

"Remember he always said, 'True power comes from within.' And that 'the ultimate mastering comes not from the body, but from the mind'? He really taught those Ninja Turtles some cool ways to deal with pain and obstacles."

"So…?"

"Well, talking to Flora is sort of like that; you really learn things. It opens your eyes and allows you to see—almost like a picture but in words—how you can do better in a variety of ways. Like how you talk to people, or maybe why people don't seem to like you, or why you lose your temper. That sort of thing."

"OK, Dad…" Sam murmured.

Maria's enthusiasm was palpable, as was Sam's indifference. Yet, somehow, all three of them seemed a little brighter. They were engaging with one another and didn't fall into their typical evasive and short-tempered patterns. As Carl looked across the table through the amber glow of the candles, Maria was smiling at Sam. How small he still seemed, a baby in many ways, even though adolescence had already reared its ugly head.

The whole evening was pleasant…*pleasant*! Later that evening, Carl was eager to write in his notebook about how he felt.

*Tonight was nice. It would be so good to feel at peace in my home again. This is what I need—a sanctuary. Not another battleground.*

Carl recalled a line from a book he'd read by Richard Bach when he was dating Maria… What was it? Something to the effect of, "You can never wish for something without the power to make it happen." *I just hope I have the strength of character to see this thing through,* he wrote. Then he thought of another saying he had loved and memorized from that same long-forgotten book. He wrote it as the last line of the entry in his notebook.

*"Argue for your limitations, and sure enough, they're yours."*

◆

The freezing rain was bitingly cold. It came pouring down hard, like tiny brittle shards of glass that shattered as they hit the trees and the rooftops of cars. Employees began running inside from all corners of the parking lot, holding briefcases and handbags over their heads for cover.

Carl had gotten to work early. He'd heard the weather report and anticipated that the freezing rain would delay him, and he had to meet with Jake on another project update. More delays. The thought of it made him queasy. Was it nervousness or shame, he wondered—or a combination of both? He had really lost it the last time he met with Jake, and Carl hoped his buttons wouldn't get pushed again. As he strode down the hall to his office, he was deep in thought, reliving the last conversation he'd had with his coworker, and didn't notice Ines coming around the corner.

"Hey, Carl—how are you doing?"

"Oh! Hi, Ines…great. How are you?"

"Doing well, thanks. I wanted to ask you how things were

going with Flora?"

"You know what…I'm surprised how well it's going. I'm really learning a lot. I have to admit I wasn't sure about this whole thing, but I'm finding it a real eye-opener. I'm enjoying the process—I'm actually meeting with her again tomorrow."

"That's great. I'm so happy to hear it. If there's anything you need on my end, don't hesitate to ask."

"Thanks very much, Ines. And thank you for the opportunity."

Ines smiled as she walked down to her office. *Wow, he really seems to be doing better…*

◆

The scent of coffee brewing was almost hypnotic. Carl poured a mug from the pot to galvanize him for his meeting with Jake. He deliberately got to the boardroom earlier than their scheduled meeting; he wanted to be ready and settled in before Jake got there. As he rounded the corner, he could see Jake was already seated and looking over some notes.

*Shoot! He beat me to it!*

Why did this irk him so much, he wondered. He could already feel his neck getting stiffer and his jaw clenching in anticipation. His chest tightened slightly as he opened the door of the boardroom.

"Jake." Carl nodded toward him.

"Hey," Jake muttered, without looking up from his notes.

"So I got your message—what's happening with the Brookstone project?"

"I really don't know what to tell you, Carl. The installers are behind schedule and there's been another problem with the color on the back-painted glass," Jake said in a monotone. "The architects keep sending us new samples every day to try and match—but they're never satisfied. I feel like they're trying to bill more hours, and they're driving us crazy at the same time."

"What do you mean, you don't know what to tell me?" Carl had his hands on the desk and began to feel like he wanted to pound his fists on the table, but he resisted and placed them on his lap instead.

*What is it about this guy that gets to me every time?*

Jake brought Carl up to speed on the production and installation issues on the project, barely making eye contact. It was all Carl could do not to lose it again, but he held back. It wasn't easy—Jake had no regard for what was important, that was evident. Clearly neither one wanted to have to deal with the other, and they ended the meeting with no solid plan to rectify the problems at hand.

◆

Carl went back to his office, deflated. How could he have felt so positive about things barely forty-five minutes ago? Would he ever get a handle on this problem with Jake? Why did Jake trigger him like that? He felt himself drifting back into a coil of worry, stress and anger. He tried to think of something positive…well, at least he felt good about keeping his irritation with Jake a little more in check than usual during the meeting.

He picked up his cell phone and looked up Joe's number. Maybe he could help shed some light on the situation.

◆

The next day, Carl was ready for his meeting with Flora. The night before, he had written in his notebook for well over an hour. Maria noticed him writing furiously at the kitchen table and went upstairs to have a bath, deciding it best to leave him alone with his thoughts. He brought the notes he had made to the meeting to discuss them with Flora—he really needed some insight.

The sun's shadows undulated over the fireplace mantle in Flora's waiting area. Carl took a deep breath as he read through the points in his notebook.

Flora's office door opened. "Come on in, Carl."

"I see you have some notes there?"

"Yes. Unfortunately, I didn't have such a great day at work yesterday...I was really triggered...and I wanted to try to make sense of things before our meeting."

"That's great that you took the time to write about it, Carl. I commend you on your dedication. It's not an easy thing to do when you are feeling upset. Tell me more about this feeling of being triggered."

"OK, well I had to meet with Jake again—the coworker that I had a run-in with that started this whole process. I could feel that tension even before I got into the meeting room, as though I was right back there."

"Back where?"

"Back in the mire of our last argument. It was like it never left me and was just lurking somewhere inside... That's one of the things I wrote in my notebook."

"Can you elaborate on that, Carl?"

"Well, it wasn't just the emotions of frustration, anger and resentment—there were physical things too."

"OK, what physical things?"

"Like before I went into the meeting, my neck became tight and I felt hot, like the blood was rushing to my head—and my jaw hurt from clenching. Even when I tried to relax, it just kept coming back, uncontrollably."

"Then what happened?"

"Well, the meeting wasn't great. We barely made eye contact and we didn't really collaborate to solve the issue. I'm worried that if we don't get together on a solution soon it could cause us to blow the project—or maybe even lose the client."

Flora looked up from her notes. "I'm so sorry. We will get this sorted out. Let's talk about your emotional and physical reactions. Did they feel appropriate given the situation?"

"Well, no, actually. They felt like leftovers."

"Leftovers?"

"Yes, it was like they weren't coming from the current situation. I mean, things are still not great between us, but if I hadn't felt the leftover feelings from our last argument, I might have been able to hear him out better, and we could have worked on a solution together."

"That's great insight, Carl. And I see what you mean about 'leftovers.' I like that analogy. If I may, I'd like to tell you a little bit about physical and emotional reactions that, in some cases, seem out of context. We all experience the world through the lens of our unique life experiences combined with individual differences in the strength of our feelings. Our responses, both physical and emotional, are influenced by all of these factors. We refer to this as 'affect intensity.' "

"OK…"

"This is a very complex topic, but put simply, it influences the intensity of the emotions we feel in response to typical life events—and it differs for each person. Given that each person is unique, some feel things more intensely than others do. If you think about heat emitting from a stove, to you it may seem warm, whereas someone else may experience it as hot. So it's having that appreciation for individual differences, an understanding that to some, the stove is warm; to others, the stove is hot. This understanding and acceptance leads to more compassion for others, as well."

"So that's why something Maria gets very emotionally upset about may not even phase me…or why I get tight as a drum and red-faced when dealing with Jake, who is so nonchalant about problems that I think he should take more seriously?"

"Well, that's an interesting observation, Carl. Could you expand on that for me?"

"Sure. Well, I guess it just hit me now, as you were explaining that intensity thing, that one of the reasons I get so over-the-top with Jake is that when he runs into difficulties, he never really reacts. He just delivers the bad news and shrugs it off. It feels like he's not invested."

"Invested?"

◆

"Like he doesn't care, I guess."

"Well," Flora countered, "is it possible that Jake is just not a very emotional person—about anything?"

"It's possible...I suppose." Carl stopped and thought for a moment. "You know, I do notice that he doesn't react strongly to the good stuff either—like when we win business or a job gets an award."

"You just presented us both with a perfect example of affect intensity, Carl. It's like the volume on a radio—there are 'high volume' and 'low volume' people. And to your point about Jake, affect intensity can definitely be associated with something positive or negative."

"Hmm, I guess my affect intensity is a little high—at least on the negative side of things."

"We can work on that, not to worry. What we need to focus on is helping you to develop new skills and try different approaches. One thing I'd like you to consider is mindfulness meditation."

"I'm not sure about that...it seems a little...out there."

"Mindfulness meditation along with some of the other skills I'd like to go over with you can really help you experience emotions with more equanimity."

"OK, now you lost me."

"Equanimity refers to balance. It's simply the acceptance of 'what is' without attachment—along with a healthy dose of self-control. When we are operating with more equanimity, we are more sensitive to the fact that we all see the world from a different perspective, a totally different vantage point. And from their point of view, they are not seeing what's at stake the way you do. So if we judge them for not seeing what we see, that judgment is not helpful in reaching our goal, which is alignment. We might completely disagree with how they see the world, but we can still respect that they are acting authentically. When we remain in equanimity, that task is a lot easier to do. In fact, it changes your entire perspective."

"So how do I stay in equanimity?"

"There are a few ways, but that's why I want you to consider mindfulness meditation as it's one of the most helpful ways to develop more balance emotionally, which can also help support you in feeling more physically stable."

Carl smirked. "So do I have to sit cross-legged on the floor and do a chant?"

"No, of course not. Mindfulness meditation can be done sitting, lying down, even while walking. And, no, you don't have to chant—unless that's your thing." Flora smiled.

"We carry such heavy baggage in the form of our past

disappointments, emotional pain and anger," Flora went on. "Meditation is a way to let these things go—with regular practice, it is possible—so that our buttons are not being pushed as much."

"I do need to learn to let things go a little more, that's for sure."

"The other thing to integrate is focus on the breath. When we focus our attention and concentration on the breath, we calm the body, which in turn, calms the mind. This shifts us into equanimity, allowing us to perceive and sense things in a more balanced way. It also helps us stay in the moment. It's an excellent tool to use because we cannot escape it. We all have to breathe, right here and right now."

"That's for sure!" Carl laughed. "Well, I have to change something. Things aren't working for me as they are now."

"OK, I'll give you some ideas to help you get started and a few apps you can try, as well."

"Thanks. I was also wondering how you will let Maria and Sam know about their results—by email?"

"Actually, I don't usually do this, but I could go over the results with all three of you here as a family."

"Really? That sounds great, thank you!"

"Yes. As I say, it's a little unusual for me, but I will do it in

◆

this instance. I want to help."

◆

It was still light outside as Carl got in the car to go meet Joe. He was really excited to tell his old friend and mentor about all this. Of course Joe would love the idea of meditation…

He looked down at one of the pages Flora had given him to read on mindfulness meditation as well as some quotes from a book by Thich Nhat Hanh. One of the passages stood out to him:

*When we see the top of a tree being tossed about in a storm, we have the feeling that the tree may be blown down at any moment. But if we look at the trunk of the tree, we will see it's very steady, and we know the tree will stand strong…*

*A strong emotion is like a storm, and can do a lot of damage. We need to know how to protect ourselves and create a safe environment where we can weather the storm. Keeping our body and mind safe from the storm is our practice. After each storm, we will become stronger, more solid and less fearful of the storms. We can learn to take care of the painful feelings and strong emotions emerging from the depth of our consciousness. Each time a storm comes up sit quietly and return to your breathing and your body. Turn your attention away from whatever it is that you believe*

◆

*is the source of suffering and instead focus on your breathing. Mindful breathing is your anchor in the storm. Remind yourself, "I have passed through many storms. Every storm has to pass; no storm stays forever. This state of mind will pass..."*

Carl looked up into the tree canopy in the parking lot. The wind was wafting softly through the pines. He found himself staring at them; the gentle swells of their feathery fronds looked soothing. He drew in a deep breath and let it go, slowly, before turning on the ignition and driving out of the parking lot.

# CHAPTER SEVEN

As Carl pulled up in front of Joe's house, he realized he needed to address the elephant in the room—he wasn't going to pretend it didn't exist any longer. He had decided not to broach the subject of his father until now, but his work with Flora made him actually *want* to tackle it. He felt very close to Joe and didn't want to have this issue hanging over their heads. Besides, he desperately needed Joe's advice.

Carl wanted to get Joe's opinion about what to do, even if he wouldn't like what he would hear. Funny how this work had him wanting to face these daunting issues instead of hiding from them.

The wooden shutters that lined the windows of Joe's home were open, and Carl could see Joe working in the kitchen. He rang the bell, and almost immediately, the door flung open wide as Joe stood to one side gesturing with a grandiose sweep of his arm. "Entrée, monsieur," he said with a grin. Carl could smell Joe's "famous" chai and the sweet aroma of something freshly baked.

Carl sniffed the air. "What…is that?"

"Lemon oat scones."

"Oh man…you're killing me. My mouth is watering already!"

"Good! Pull up a chair in the sunroom, and I'll be right there with a whole tray of them!"

Carl felt a sense of easy warmth with Joe. Nothing feigned, no uncomfortable silences—just ease. Joe felt like something of a hybrid to Carl: part brother, friend, father, and spiritual mentor. He laughingly referred to him as Yoda on occasion. Yet, none of these multiple roles ever seemed to confine the others.

Carl relaxed into a worn leather chair and basked in the sunlight streaming through the windows. "Wow, you'd almost think the weather was pleasant out there," Carl said loudly, so Joe could hear him in the kitchen.

Joe rattled into the room with a metal tray of scones and

steaming mugs of chai and placed them on a small coffee table. "Yes! Spring is on the way. I hear more birds these days too."

"Service! Thanks, Joe!"

"Fresh baked! My usual Sunday indulgence—nice to share it with you, Carl." Joe smiled.

"So, what's new?"

"Well…a few things…but I wanted to ask you something first."

"OK, shoot."

"Well…what can you tell me about my dad? Have you been in touch?"

"I was wondering when you would want to discuss that, but I was waiting for you to decide it was time. Yes, as a matter of fact, I saw him a week or so ago. How about you?"

"What about me?"

Joe looked up from his tea and met Carl's eyes. "Don't you think it's time you considered getting over there for a visit? I'm not sure how long he has…"

"I don't even know what to say to him anymore, Joe. I know it's the right thing to do, considering his diagnosis, but he said so many hurtful things—things that just can't be unsaid. He was so accusatory…and incredibly spiteful."

Joe hesitated and then spoke slowly. "I'm sure you've heard

that Buddhist saying, 'Holding on to anger is like grasping a hot coal with the intent of throwing it at someone else—' "

"Yes, I know the rest," Carl interjected. " 'You are the one who gets burned,' right?"

"Right. So if you accept that as truth, then you have to let go—and forgive him—before it's too late."

"But how? The way we left things was pretty horrible. And I certainly don't feel like I have to apologize for anything."

"You start at the beginning, Carl. Just get over there and be with him. Don't try to talk things out at first—just be there for him. Eventually you will make peace, somehow. If the intent is there, the way will present itself. If you don't try, there's a good chance you will regret it."

Joe was right—no question. But Carl had to think about this. Even though his father was dying of stage IV cancer, he still couldn't get over how his father had berated him—and insulted his family in front of the relatives and close friends who were visiting that Thanksgiving weekend more than five years ago.

Joe did his best to provide Carl with insight into his father's psyche and how the disease affected his emotions, and he spoke further about forgiveness and regret.

"You know, Carl, it's very possible the cancer had already

affected his neurological system, even back then, considering his exposure to chemical warfare. Vietnam was a pretty horrific time in our lives."

"Yes, I guess it's possible…sounds like an excuse though."

"Your father may never admit to making a mistake. He may not even realize he should ask for forgiveness. So you'll have to be the change in your relationship and find it in your heart to forgive him, for selfish reasons."

"Selfish reasons?"

"Yes, for your own sanity and well-being. How would you feel if something happened and you hadn't tried to connect with him and bury the hatchet in your own way? It might haunt you for the rest of your life. You know what they say…"

"What's that?"

"This is not word for word, but it's something like, 'We ourselves must walk the path; no one saves us but ourselves.' "

"I know. I promise to give it some more thought, Joe. I know I have to do something soon—if, in fact, I decide to see him."

Carl sat back and looked out the window for a moment. The brilliant sun was gone, trading golden warmth for gray stillness.

Joe shifted gears. "So, tell me, what's happening with your coach?"

"Oh, it's great, Joe. I'm really learning some interesting things about myself. Lots of light bulbs going off, and I'm journaling more," he said, smiling. "Flora is really educating me about my emotional approaches and personality and how that shows up in all my relationships. I took this online assessment that pinpoints your emotional type and dialogue style. And I'm using mindfulness meditation now, as well. Flora gave me some information about it, and I've been doing it religiously every day. I never thought I'd say this, but I love it! It calms me down a lot."

Joe smiled widely. "You have learned well, Grasshopper. Seriously though, that's terrific! So are things getting better at work?"

"Well...that's the thing...although I am learning more and more about what makes me tick, and I've started meditating, I'm still having these knee-jerk reactions with this guy at work who seems to constantly push my buttons."

"What is the learning there, Carl?"

"Learning...? I really don't know. All I've learned is he is driving me insane."

"Whatever—or in this case whoever—pushes our buttons is said to be our greatest teacher."

"Well, there must be *some* major kind of lesson to learn then, because my blood pressure literally goes up twenty points around him!" Carl chuckled.

"When do you see Flora again?"

"This week. Actually, she is allowing Maria and Sam to take the assessment so that we can all learn about our dialogue styles and how they affect our communication and relationships. She doesn't usually do that, but she's making an exception for us—which is really cool."

"Well that should be interesting! You'll have to fill me in."

"Definitely."

◆

Wednesday afternoon, Carl left the office early and drove to the train to pick up Maria and Sam. The three rode in silence to Flora's office. By 3:45, they were seated in the waiting area: Maria flipping through a magazine, Carl checking his email and Sam scrolling through social media. Just a little before 4:00, Flora came through the main door.

"Good afternoon, everyone! Just give me a minute to hang up my coat, and we can get started!"

Carl and Maria stood up and started walking slowly toward the office door. "Sam, come on," Maria said in a loud whisper.

Flora motioned them toward the sofa. "Please take off your coats and get comfortable," Flora said as the three sat down on the sofa.

Flora noticed that Sam was still scrolling through his social media feed, head down, still wearing his coat. "Sam, would it be OK if you put your phone away while we are here together?" Flora asked. Sam looked up with an exasperated expression and put his phone back in his coat pocket.

Maria looked over at her son. "Sam…coat."

"OK, OK," he said under his breath as he shrugged off his jacket.

Flora began, "Well it's great to see all of you here today. This is not something I usually do, but I felt it would be helpful. So here we are…and how are all of you feeling about this?"

"Well, I'm happy to explore different communication styles and how we can understand each other better," Maria offered.

"That's great, Maria. Carl, what about you? I think you felt it might be enlightening for the three of you to learn more about the results of one another's assessments and how your varying profiles can incite certain issues at home."

Carl took a deep breath before answering. "Yes, and I know that I've definitely been part of the problem when things haven't gone well at home." He looked first to his wife and then over to his son. "I take full responsibility for my actions, and I just want to say to you both that I know I've been a bit of a jerk lately…and I'm sorry."

Flora felt a difference in the air, as if a powerful shift had just jolted through the room. *What a change! Going from feeling like everything was everyone else's fault to this...?* This was what it was all about. This was why she was dedicated to this work.

Sam spoke first. "Yeah, Dad, you have been pretty hard to deal with. But at least you admit it."

"I know, Sam. I'm trying to change that." Carl felt grateful in that moment that he had arrived at this point. That he wasn't just reacting—he was actually thinking rationally and not regretting his words as soon as they tumbled out of his mouth. He was trying. He was making progress.

Maria smiled and nodded knowingly. "Sam, I think your dad is doing much better. We have to encourage each other, right?"

"That is true, Maria. Well, it might be helpful for us to look at the results at this point." Flora ventured, "Shall we? Maria, your results were very high on the Interdependent type. The Interdependent person operates with a spirit of collaboration, so it's important to you to establish a win-win relationship with others."

"I can see that." Maria nodded. "Go on."

"So your main concern is your relationships, and your

decisions, actions and agreements are based on balance for all parties involved. You don't really concern yourself with being right, necessarily, and you only feel victorious if everyone else feels that way. This personality type remains interested in, and curious about, the needs of other people and invites others to understand their own needs, as well. Which is wonderful!"

"Until it isn't?" Maria smirked.

"Well, yes. Like all the profiles, when they are balanced, there are many positives, but when out of balance, it can cause problems. In your case, if your Interdependent approach becomes intense, you can exhaust yourself and others around you because you might insist on hashing everything out in the name of closure."

"So I may have trouble letting go?"

"Yes, if the approach is too intense," Flora replied. "So you might say, 'OK, so neither one of us is happy with this situation, but let's see where we can take it. Let's see how far we can move that needle. Fifty-one percent is better than fifty. I'm willing to give up some things if you are, so we can achieve a better outcome.' " Flora paused. "Do you see where I'm going with this?"

"I think so." Maria nodded.

"There are times when you overvalue that consensus and try a little too hard to make something work for everyone involved. But as I say, when this approach is balanced it is very collaborative, which is a good thing."

Flora looked over at Carl. "Your husband, on the other hand, operates quite differently. He scored very high in the Directive style, and his second most prominent score was Diligent."

"Yes, he told me all about his results—and I couldn't agree more. I find it fascinating, because we all handle the same things so differently, and we can't see eye to eye in some cases because of our different styles, but we have to keep trying to get to a middle ground."

"Exactly, Maria! That's a great example of your Interdependent style, and your personality type can be very helpful in that sense."

Flora looked over at Sam. She smiled and hesitated before speaking. "Would you like to know your results, Sam?"

Sam shrank further back into the sofa and grabbed a cushion, holding it on his lap. "I *guess* so."

"OK. Just stop me if there's anything you want me to explain further. Your interpersonal dialogue style is Harmonious and Cautious, so you tend to avoid conversations, particularly when you are upset or something is bothering you. Does that sound right to you?"

Sam looked away for a moment and then looked back at

Flora. "Well, I guess…"

"The Harmonious and Cautious style is great in one sense because you are a peacemaker, and sometimes you even put your own needs aside to make others happy. But putting your own needs aside means you can feel resentful or taken advantage of on occasion. The cautious aspect of your profile relates to keeping things to yourself, not letting others know things until you are sure you can trust their reaction or figure out the outcome. Does this make sense?"

Sam fidgeted and then his face flooded with color.

Maria turned to her son and reached out to touch his arm. "What is it, Sam?"

"Well…I didn't want to say anything, but I have been holding something inside for a while," he stammered.

"Sam, honey, what is it?"

"It's OK, Mom, it's just something that happened at school—well, not *at* school, online."

Maria began to sit forward on the sofa, her face furrowed with concern. "Sam, please tell us what happened so we can help."

"It was just these kids who made fun of me…and made me look really stupid. But it went on for a long time."

"How long?" Flora asked softly.

"About two months altogether. But it's over now."

"Oh...for...I can't believe this," Carl said incredulously. "Why didn't you tell us? Every time I tried to talk to you, you shut me out. I knew something was wrong!"

"Because, Dad, you were so wrapped up in...whatever you were wrapped up in," Sam shot back. "And you were always so grouchy and short with me and Mom... I just didn't want to put this on you. And, Mom, you always seemed so worried about Dad and his moods. I didn't want to add to whatever was going on."

Maria felt tears well up in her eyes but fought them back. "Sam, *you* are our priority. There is nothing more important than what's going on with you, especially if you are struggling. We could have helped you...I wish you had told us. You must have felt so alone!"

"It's OK, Mom. It's over now...everything has cooled off. Those kids have probably moved on to bugging somebody else now. I just avoid them."

Carl turned to face Sam. "Son, I'm so sorry I wasn't there for you when you needed me most. That's going to change, I promise. But you have to help us, OK? We need you to talk to us more about what's happening with you, especially when something is bothering you."

"OK, Dad, I will. But only if you promise not to be so

moody."

Carl smiled and leaned over to high-five his son. "Deal."

Flora took a deep breath. "Well, I'm very glad you had the opportunity to get this out in the open. And I'm sure you'll be talking through this at home, as well. Do you feel like you want to keep going?"

"Sure," Sam offered with a thin smile.

Flora went on to explain how each of their dialogue styles might show up at home and how that would affect their interactions with one another.

"This is great information, Flora," Maria enthused. "It's really informing us about some of our autopilot reactions to things and why we have problems communicating in some instances. Even though we are from the same family, we certainly are different!"

"Yes, I agree." Flora nodded. "We are all so very different. But once we understand those differences, we can come together in a much more elegant, aligned way. And our communication just flows better. It's important to remember that the way we show up today and tomorrow has a significant effect on our relationships and what those relationships will look like years from now."

The family thanked Flora and stepped outside to greet a

deluge of rain. "Let's make a run for it!" said Carl. "How about we go for pizza?"

Sam tugged at his father's jacket and exclaimed, "Awesome! Can we go to Bartolli's?"

"Sure—let's do it, buddy!"

# CHAPTER EIGHT

YESTERDAY'S SESSION WITH FLORA WAS *eye opening. I'm learning more about emotional resilience through meditation, and self-
care, and we discussed the fact that I'm still trying to avoid Jake
at work so that I don't get triggered. Flora helped me learn some
new techniques for the next time things get heated. She says these
techniques can help me both at work and at home. I took notes so
I could recall what was said. She called these "emotional self-regulation skills." Flora mentioned that these skills are needed to
meet my own emotional needs during times of stress, particularly
during a high-stakes conversation.*

*1. The first one was to simply pause. Instead of jumping in, like I usually do, Flora said that it's best to take a step back and avoid responding right away. It is very easy for people to react quickly to the stress they feel in the moment, she says. Basically, pausing is a great technique for building impulse control.*

*2. The next point was to focus on taking deep breaths. Flora said that taking long, slow deep breaths would allow me a few seconds to "reset" before I move forward. This takes mindful attention. The meditation will help me develop more mindfulness too.*

*3. The third point was that, in the heat of the moment, it is helpful to deflect attention from myself and onto someone or something else. I can do this by asking questions, by taking notes or by redirecting my gaze from the other person, looking briefly at an object or place in the room.*

*4. The last point Flora made was that, if necessary, I could simply delay the conversation. It's not always possible to manage emotions in the moment, so rescheduling allows a bit of time to refresh my perspective and possibly change my approach.*

Carl had gone to find his notebook in the study after everyone went to bed. He wanted to keep his thoughts fresh, so he took a few minutes to jot down some notes from his last session with Flora. They were significant points, and although he had made notes on the handout she'd given him, he wanted to expand upon them. He was really feeling that he was opening up to new constructs of thought. The way he looked at so many things was slowly changing—in a good way.

He was compelled to write a few more lines in his notebook:

*No day is perfect. It's as if we have elements of imperfection in each one in order to find the beauty in the next. Nothing is guaranteed beyond the present moment. Find the learning in each day, no matter how difficult.*

*What you resist, persists.*

Carl paused for a moment and reread his entry before closing the notebook. *Who is this person?* He chuckled to himself. It was interesting to him that what he wrote was a reflection of what had happened ever since he'd started working with Flora. Maybe he was waking up…

He realized that as long as he resisted change, obviously, nothing was *ever* going to get better.

◆

Carl got to work early Monday morning. He planned to get a jump on emails and project check-ins before putting some time aside to plan for the next quarter. He was confident that with his hard-won skills he learned with Flora, he could improve his financial situation as well as his communication.

## Emotional Self-Regulation Skills

Four skills and techniques needed to meet **your emotional needs.**

### 1. Pause.

Avoid responding immediately; pause first. Pausing is an excellent technique for building impulse control.

### 2. Take deep breaths.

Pay attention to your breathing. Take long, slow, deep breaths, and then go forward.

### 3. Deflect attention.

It is helpful to deflect attention or energy away from ourselves and to someone or something else. Ask questions, take notes or redirect your gaze from the person you are speaking with, to an object or place in the room.

### 4. Delay if needed (reschedule, refresh or reset).

It is not always possible to manage our feelings in the present moment. If required, consider delaying the conversation altogether. The delay could take minutes, hours or days.

◆

He opened up his email to see a note from Jake.

*Carl, there's a problem with the New York job. The paint for the stained glass pieces is not compatible with the faux lead. Trying to work it out. Project delayed by 3-4 weeks. Please inform the client.*

Carl was furious. *Damn!* The architect involved in this was very high profile, and he had more work for Solar—a refurbishment of the airport. How could this be happening again? His fingers hovered over the keyboard. Carl was just about to type how frustrated he was and ask why Jake hadn't known this before. This was so typical of him...and now it fell into Carl's lap, once again. And sending him an email instead of discussing it directly...what was that about?

OK... *Pause. Breathe. Deflect. Delay.*

He stopped, put his hands beside him on the chair and focused on his breath. In and out slowly... He looked at the family photo on his desk, away from the computer screen. As he sat there, he thought about two outcomes of his possible actions. One, after he sent an angry reply to the email. And the other, if he went to him and coolly addressed the situation. He was determined to remain calm, and he sat for several moments before he got up and walked slowly down the hall to Jake's office.

Jake was bent over some plans, in a hushed discussion with

one of his technicians.

"Hi, Jake, I got your email. Geez, what a mess."

"Well, you take these things on and don't even consult with us first, Carl. What do you expect? It's always on us to make good on your unrealistic promises." Jake sighed dramatically.

Carl stopped and said nothing. He knew if he reacted to Jake, they would go right back to their same acrimonious pattern. He felt his heart rate go up. *Slow deep breaths, in and out.*

Carl needed a moment to cool off before speaking. He wandered over to another set of plans for a housing project from a sales manager. "This looks pretty ambitious." He then turned to Jake, feeling a little more composed. "Look, Jake, I know the timeframe on this was tight, but it's all I could do to stretch it this far. We can't go back to the architect at this point and tell him that his general contractor will just have to wait around doing nothing for three to four weeks while he waits for this delivery. That would be financial suicide. The penalties would discount any margin of profit. What can we do to work together on this? I'm willing to help," Carl offered.

"You just don't understand my world, Carl. And it makes me mad that you think you can just waltz in here and try to get me to agree to your unreasonable demands. You just don't get it…"

Carl felt himself getting aggravated. "We *all* have our

problems, Jake."

"Some more than others, Carl," Jake said cynically under his breath.

*What the hell does he mean by that? That I have problems? What the...? This guy is just the biggest jerk!*

Carl stopped and took a deep breath. "I have to get to a meeting, Jake. Can we talk about this on Thursday? We have to figure out a plan."

"Whatever, Carl," Jake said, without looking up.

Carl walked down the hall and stepped outside into the fresh air. *Deep breaths, in and out... Well, at least I didn't think about throwing a chair at him this time...*

He *had* to figure out what was triggering him with Jake.

◆

Carl was late for his meeting with Flora. It seemed as though every Tuesday he had to deal with a million disjointed issues. "Troubled Tuesday," he called it. And on top of that, there was an ice storm—in late April! He flipped on the radio for a weather update.

"As much of Chicagoland was able to wait out the damaging impact from a historic ice storm over the weekend and into Monday, lingering effects are still causing major concerns on

Chicago-area roads. Freezing rain and rainfall warnings stretch across the region with the threat for treacherous travel on poorly drained roads and highways. School closures and bus cancellations are widespread and more wintry weather, including ice pellets and rain, will persist throughout this week."

*Just great…*

Carl pulled into the parking lot of Flora's office just as another deluge threatened. Lightning streaked through the storm clouds furrowed in a foreboding sky. Deep in thought about what he wanted to say to Flora, Carl sprinted across the wet pavement, the swirling water seeping into the soles of his shoes.

He wanted to tell Flora about Jake's undermining tactics and the incompetence…the utter ineptitude of the guy. *Why does he get to me like this?*

As he reached the double glass doors of the building, he grabbed the metal handle and pulled. His hand slithered off the icy surface, and he fell backward onto the pavement, catching himself with his right arm to break the fall. "*Ahhh…*" Carl bellowed. He got up slowly, recognizing that the pavement around him had become a frozen menace. He slid across the sidewalk, ever so cautiously, toward the door and managed to get it open without falling. He limped up the steps to see Flora standing at the top of the stairs.

"Oh no...are you all right, Carl? I thought I heard you yell—it looks like you had a bit of a spill. The temperature must have plunged. There's salt out there all over the pavement, but with all the rain and then the sudden freezing..."

"It's OK, I'm fine." He sighed. "Though, admittedly, I've had better days," he managed. He took off his coat and sat down on the sofa in Flora's office.

"Can I get you anything, Carl?"

"No, let's just get started. I've got something I really need to get off my chest."

"OK, why don't you tell me about it."

"Well, the skills you taught me last week, the self-regulation techniques?"

"Yes."

"I've been using them—at home—and found them to be helpful in keeping my hot head in check. I'm finding that the techniques are good for my relationship with Maria—and particularly helpful with Sam. I'm not jumping in to 'fix' things when they talk to me. Instead, I'm listening more, doing the breathing, deflecting when things get tense...that sort of thing."

"That's great, Carl. How about at work?"

"Well, that's what I wanted to talk to you about. Yesterday, I met with Jake briefly. There's another major issue at work with yet another complicated project, and I went to him to try to figure out a solution. This was after he sent me an *email* to let me know about the problem."

"How did that go?"

"Unfortunately, not well. Though I have to admit, the self-regulation techniques helped me keep my anger in check, which is a good thing. And I was able to deflect a bit, when I wanted to explode. And then I delayed the conversation because he was really badgering me — it was as if he *wanted* me to lose it."

"As difficult as that may have been, Carl, you really have made progress if you were able to do all of those things when you perceived Jake to be pushing your buttons."

"Perceived? No, he was definitely trying to get my goat. No question."

"Well, let me ask you this then, Carl. You want to get past these issues with Jake, right?"

"I have to if things are going to get better at work—that's why we started working together."

"Of course. So what do you think it would take to shift the dynamic with Jake?"

"I really don't know yet…but I do know that it has to change."

"Good. Do you think Jake is intentionally trying to hurt

you or sabotage the projects?"

"Well, there are moments…" Carl paused, took a deep breath and let it out before continuing. "No, I guess he isn't. He most likely wants to keep his job and do it well—just like all of us, I suppose."

"Right. So if Jake's *intention* is not to hurt you or the project, is it possible for you to forgive him? Could you put the past aside and give him the benefit of the doubt? Remember, I'm referring to his *intention* not his *behavior.* The two are very different. We can more easily excuse poor behavior than we can forgive cruel intention."

"Hmmm. Maybe…"

"You mentioned in another session that when you met with Jake, the feelings you had didn't seem appropriate to the situation at hand. You said your feelings felt like leftovers, remember? Like they were old feelings, relating to other incidents in the past. That's what seems to be constant in this situation."

Carl nodded his head in agreement.

"Think of it this way—if you remain in history, nothing changes. If you can remove the past from your memory and reframe your thoughts around your relationship with Jake—and I'm not saying it's necessarily easy to let go of the past, but it's really the only way to improve things—and commit to approaching

♦

the situation in a new way, you might see him differently."

"How so?"

"My guess is that Jake feels just as much tension and angst around you as you do around him. Let me ask you this: Can you tell me anything positive about Jake?"

Carl looked out the window and then turned back to Flora. "Well, when he's on track, he can really be creative. He's a good problem solver...and I think he might be a good project manager."

"Really? That's very positive. I'm sure those attributes may not be at the forefront at this juncture, considering the animosity between you, but they're there waiting for you, Carl."

"Waiting for me?"

"Imagine, for a moment, if your relationship with Jake was working. How would he be able to assist you in these complex issues with your 'problem projects'?"

Carl thought about it for a moment. "Well...he might be able to come up with a technical or creative solution."

He thought about it further. "He might also try to get extra people in the factory on board to move the job through quicker. And he might be more helpful, instead of trying to fight me at every turn."

"Excellent." Flora smiled. "Perhaps it's now time to talk

◆

about how you can manage the emotions of another person during a heated conversation. That might be really helpful for you in this situation."

"How to manage the emotions of another person? That sounds odd. We can only manage our own emotions, correct?"

"Actually, there are quite a few ways to accomplish this—if you remain mindful and possess the necessary tools for managing the emotions of others while interacting with them."

"I'm all ears." Carl smiled.

"OK, first of all, during a heated or high-stakes conversation, you need to be sure to *maintain* or *enhance* the self-regard of the other person. And you need to be aware of the difference between the two approaches. You would try to *maintain* self-regard of the person when they doubt themselves or when they're experiencing challenging situations. But you would try to *enhance* self-regard when they have accomplished something special or unique—or when it's important for them to recognize their value."

"I can see how this could be used effectively with Sam," Carl observed.

"That's right. As would the next step: actively and mindfully listening. Pretty straightforward. Truly listen to what the person is saying; don't jump in with a solution. Actively listen, focusing on the person's words and the emotion attached to those words—and be mindful of your response to them."

"OK...we both know I tend to jump in pretty quickly..."

"What you have to remember is that the other person needs to feel they have been *heard*. Which brings me to the third step: empathy. When you respond to the person with empathy, you are allowing them to feel safe in the conversation. You have to resist trying to get in there and solve their problems or to tell them what to do. You have to empathize instead."

"What's the problem with someone trying to solve another person's problem? Aren't you trying to help by doing that?"

Flora paused for a moment and went on. "It's not quite that simple. The short answer is, you don't solve the other person's problem *for* them; you solve it *together*. It can also be disrespectful to believe that you have all the answers to that person's particular issue—and it's not addressing what's really going on with them."

"Eyes officially opened on that one." Carl smiled. "Anything else?"

"Yes, the last point is to invite participation. So you don't bark orders or make decisions of your own accord; you have to *invite* the person to actively participate in the discussion as well as the resolution."

"I can see how that would work well and create more of a partnership."

"Yes, it does. Flora paused and then looked up from her notes at Carl. "I wonder if you would be open to an exercise that might help you to feel more empathy for Jake."

"How do you fake empathy for a guy who you feel antagonism toward? I am not sure faking compassion toward Jake is the best idea, if for no other reason than he will likely recognize that I don't really mean it."

"I think there have been times during our sessions that I've asked you to take a bit of a leap of faith." Flora smiled. "This is another one of those times. Would you agree to try something and see how it goes?"

"Yes, sure."

"Great! The exercise is called *Gratitude to Release Enmity*—or hostility. I have a copy of it for you, but let's try it quickly before you leave."

"OK."

"First, you take a few deep breaths, then relax your eyelids and smile softly. This may seem a little strange at first, but this tactic is important as it positively alters your mood state."

Flora went on. "Visualize the person you are focusing on feeling grateful for, then repeat the following sequence three

## Emotional Management Techniques (EMTs)

These are the techniques we use to successfully facilitate **the emotions of others** during a high-stakes conversation.

### 1. Enhance and Maintain Self-Regard
To affirm and retain a sense of dignity. Requires sincere gratitude, and a demonstration of respect for the other person's time, attention, beliefs, and feelings.

### 2. Active and Mindful Listening
Dedicated, fully present, and single-minded concentration while the other person is speaking. Mindful listening requires that we wait for the person to completely finish each thought, and to offer verbal and non-verbal cues that convey full attention.

### 3. Empathetic Responding
Expressions of genuine understanding of how another person is feeling, and reflecting that back to them.

### 4. Inviting Participation
This is the use of direct and encouraging verbal invitations for the other person to respond, and to offer their ideas, perspectives, and feedback, throughout the conversion.

times in your mind, taking one full breath between each line. You start with the person's name…and it goes like this:

*Jake,*
*I wish you to be well.*
*I wish you to be happy.*
*I wish you to be safe.*
*I thank you for helping me to see myself in a new light.*
*I thank you for helping me to become a much stronger, kinder and more successful person in my life journey.*

"We can wish each challenging person who crosses our path to be well, to be happy, to be safe and to find joyful meaning and purpose in this life. And if you find this exercise difficult—in other words, if you have a lot of trouble offering positive wishes sincerely—then it's a sign that you really need to do it! Keep in mind that the other person likely feels the same way you do and that they are also in need of moving past these difficult feelings," Flora explained.

"Well, I will definitely try this. It is a little 'out there'… But honestly, I have to change this dynamic between me and Jake."

"Yes, absolutely! And there's one more skill set I'd like to teach you, but we're out of time for today. When is your next meeting with Jake?"

"Well, I was so worked up, I *delayed* the conversation, actually. I put it off until Thursday. But as it turns out, Jake emailed me that he can't meet with me for a few weeks. His production schedule is jammed, and he has two of his people out on an installation in New York—so I have some time to get ready for our next encounter." Carl smiled.

"OK, good. Excellent follow-through on the emotional self-regulation skills, by the way. Here is a handout with the four emotional management techniques for your 'homework' that we just went through, as well as the gratitude exercise."

Flora stood up and said, "Now, I'm just wondering…is it possible for you to make it in for another session soon? I know your next meeting is a few weeks out, but I have one more segment to teach you, as I mentioned, that could really help. If you are able to make it in say, two weeks from today, I think you'll have all the tools you need to see a seismic shift in your relationship with Jake—and you'll likely be able to get some solutions on the table regarding these thorny project issues."

"Seismic shift? Well, sure—I'm in! Seriously, Flora, anything is better than the way we are communicating at this point—and I want to look over the emotional management techniques tonight, as well."

♦

Flora smiled and narrowed her eyes slightly. "I've got an even better idea. Read them over and try it out at home tonight with Maria…or Sam, and then let me know what happens. And I'll see you back here in two weeks—same time, same place!"

Carl felt invigorated. "Field research! I love it!"

# CHAPTER NINE

FLORA CHECKED THE TIME ON her phone as she got out of the car—8:25 a.m. Just enough time to get upstairs for her 8:30 meeting with Carl. As she strode up to the second floor, she noted he was sitting in the waiting room, deep in thought.

"Hello there! How are you on this crisp spring morning?"

He looked up to see Flora and stood up. Carl was so anxious to tell her what had happened the night before that he didn't even stop to say good morning.

"Well, it's been an eye-opening two weeks. I've been having better conversations with Maria and at work, with my clients—but I have to tell you, last night was the best part!" Carl enthused. "I used the four emotional management techniques with Sam, and it worked out really well!"

Flora beamed, motioning toward the office. "Come on in and tell me all about it!"

Carl talked quickly as he sat down and got out a notepad and pen. "It was so effective, Flora! I came home and Sam was on his phone, surfing, and I sat down to talk to him. He gave me his usual sullen responses…you know, a few grunts and groans…but I kept talking to him, and once he could see that I was really listening and fully engaged with him, he put his phone down and told me about something that was bothering him at school."

"What was that?"

"One of the teachers at school seemed to have it in for him—or at least that's how he perceived it. He said when she called on him to answer questions in class and he got something wrong, she would make a comment that was…let's just say, to his mind the comments were less than productive. In other words, the teacher didn't maintain his self-regard."

"Oh, that's not good; how did you handle the issue?"

"I started out by telling him that he was smart and hard-working—which he is—and asked if it was possible that there might be something else going on with the teacher. He wasn't too forthcoming, but I persevered. I kept talking and asked him what he thought that could be."

"And...?"

"He finally admitted that he might not have handed in a couple of his assignments on time—and that he had spoken to her in a somewhat dismissive manner a couple of times, as well."

"Well, that might do it."

"Yes, exactly. So I kept at it for a long time. I listened actively and tried to be mindful of his perspective—and his current level of maturity. I was empathetic, even though I pointed out, nicely, that we all have to meet deadlines, and if we don't, it makes people think we don't care. But then I said that I know that he truly does care about school, his marks, and what people think of him. So it really comes back to him—that he has to be more responsible. But I kept reinforcing the fact that he is usually a good student and that anything worthwhile, like school marks, takes hard work. And then I asked him if he thought that was true and he agreed—but then he added that he also felt taking responsibility for his actions was just as important. I couldn't believe it! He volunteered that himself!"

Flora beamed. "Out of the mouths of babes, as they say."

"Right! Then I asked him why he had been flippant with

♦

her, and he admitted it was because she took him to task about his late submissions in front of the 'cool kids' after school one day. He was trying to prove to them that he wasn't a weakling by answering back to her. And he was trying to be cool in front of his friends, as well."

"Well, that's bound to backfire."

"Of course. But, you know, he's learning…"

"What did you do next?"

"I just listened mindfully. I was empathetic. I would ask instead of tell, as much as possible. For instance, I asked, 'What do you think you could have done differently in that situation, Son?' Or, 'If you put yourself in her shoes, how do you think you would react if your student was careless and didn't hand in assignments on time?' He admitted he didn't think he would react any differently than his teacher did. I didn't get mad or raise my voice, and I empathized with him the whole time but didn't let him off the hook for his mistakes. I could really see him reacting differently to me. He even hugged me when our conversation ended!"

"Wow, that's great!"

"Yes! And afterwards, we brainstormed ideas on how he could improve the situation and his relationship with the teacher. I let him come up with most of the ideas, and I would just tweak them somewhat with minor suggestions. He's going to start with an apology."

"Carl, that's terrific. If you keep using the technique, you'll be amazed at how quickly your relationships can change for the better."

"I'm so grateful for this process. It's practical and creative at the same time. I think it can really help heal misunderstandings and restore failing relationships. But thank goodness my relationship with Sam is not to that point!"

"Yes, I agree, Carl. Congratulations; good work!" Flora looked up from her notes. "Now, today I want to take you even further on the learning curve, with the six-step process."

"Well, if it's anything like what I experienced last night, I'm all ears!"

"The two processes work in tandem—they are complementary. The four emotional management techniques help you manage the emotions of another during a tough conversation, and the six steps are like a map—how to get from A to B—allowing you to navigate even the most difficult conversations with ease."

"Great. I sure hope it works in my next meeting with Jake. We have definitely hit rock bottom."

"Well, let's hope so. I'll give you a printed sheet on the

---

◆

---

### The Six Steps of the
### Meaningful Alignment Process (MAP)

**PURPOSE**
1. Introduce the reason for the discussion.
2. Identify the problem, issue or opportunity.

**DISCOVERY**
3. Discuss the impact.
4. Brainstorm solutions and ideas.

**ACCOUNTABILITY**
5. Summarize actions and commit to next steps.
6. Conclude and follow up.

---

steps, but you might want to make notes as well. As you know, other things come up during sessions that you might want to recall later. OK, the first step is to introduce the reason for the discussion. This may sound like common sense, but it's so often overlooked. We've all been in meetings where we are baffled as to why we are there."

Carl nodded in agreement.

"Also, when introducing the reason for the discussion, it's

helpful to express your appreciation for the time they took to meet with you. This is particularly important if the topic you are addressing with the person is sensitive or if there has been tension in the past—as is the case with you and Jake. In this instance, opening the discussion with gratitude can be critical and can make or break the success of the interaction."

"So to recap, in my case that would be basically, 'Jake, I want to thank you for at least showing up. The reason I asked you to meet with me is to tell you what a jerk you've been.' " Carl smirked.

"Well, no, not quite." Flora smiled.

"Sorry, just being a wise guy. OK, be specific about the topic for discussion and let them know you are grateful they're meeting with you."

"Right, but let's take a step back for a moment... This reminds me to revisit the gratitude exercise with you today too. I presume you have yet to begin practicing that."

"No...not yet," Carl admitted. "I do understand how important it is to let people know that you're grateful they are meeting with you though, and it's probably even more important they can tell that you actually mean it, which is going to be a lot easier said than done when it comes to Jake."

"We will get you there, Carl, I promise. You might say,

◆

'Jake, I know you are really busy, and I appreciate you taking the time to meet today.' And remember that people can tell the degree of sincerity you have in your voice. Your gratitude and sincerity will carry over in the way you complete this first step of stating the reason for meeting with them."

Flora continued. "The second step is to identify the problem or opportunity and invite the person to share their opinions and ideas on the issue at this point as well—*before* you offer your own. While you do this, you must also bear in mind the emotional management techniques. In this case, it would be maintaining self-regard for the other person and being empathetic."

"That makes sense, I guess. By maintaining self-regard and having empathy while involving the other person in the discussion, they might be more apt to collaborate with you on a solution."

"Absolutely! Then the next step is to do with the 'whys' and 'hows.' What I'm referring to is discussing the issue's impact. At this point, you always ask the other person for their perspective on things—again, *before* you offer your own. So you might say, 'Jake, what is the impact of this situation if you and I are not able to align?' I think you'll find he will be less likely to point fingers if you approach it this way. Once he finishes offering his viewpoint, then—and only then—you offer yours."

Carl was furiously taking notes and then looked up. "OK... what's next?"

"Then you move on to brainstorming solutions to the problems together."

"I bet I'm supposed to ask Jake his ideas for solving the problem before I offer my own..." Carl smiled.

"You're really catching on now, Carl. Yes, you will gather so much information by asking Jake his thoughts before you offer your own. In a way, you get a snapshot of what is in his mind, on a silver platter. Based on what he says, it also buys you time to take a deep breath and to maintain your composure—especially if he says something that might trigger you emotionally. Throughout this process, it's important to actively and mindfully listen, as well. So put your phone or laptop away—no distractions—and really listen to what the other person is saying. Try not to focus on what you want to say in answer to their statements. If you are too focused on offering your perspective, then you are not really hearing them. And because you will have already begun your discussion from a place of sincere gratitude, listening mindfully will come a lot easier to you than you realize."

"Got it."

"Yes. And once you've both finished brainstorming

solutions, you then have to move on to accountability."

"Oh…I'm a bit worried about this step."

"Why?"

"Because of all the finger-pointing and the fact that Jake never takes responsibility for anything."

"Well, let's see what happens when you use this technique. Maybe you'll be pleasantly surprised…" Flora looked up at Carl from her notes. "Remember how high you scored on the Directive and Diligent dialogue styles?"

"Yes, I do."

"Your frustration with Jake that he 'never takes responsibility for anything' is likely to be an overreaction on your part because of how strong you are in your dominant style. You can become so attached and intensely focused on obtaining closure on challenging issues that it may be exhausting and even overwhelming to some people. Remember how Sam—whose style is highly Cautious—would shut down? And how adjusting your approach led Sam to take more responsibility for his school assignments and to see his teacher in a different light?"

"Yes, sure."

"Well, it is entirely *possible* that Jake's style is also Cautious—I'm guessing in combination with a highly Directive approach, strong enough to rival your own. The two of you are very likely to use inflexible language and carry very different perspectives into a discussion, and therefore, neither of you may be willing to let go of your respective positions. This is why following the six steps, and preparing yourself for a high-stakes conversation, mentally and emotionally, is so important."

"I can see how this would result in misunderstandings—when you consider our two dialogue styles, we're literally speaking two different languages!"

"Right. But if you stick to these steps and the emotional management techniques, you might be able to cultivate a shared language that you can both appreciate." Flora smiled. "Now let's keep going…once you've gotten to this point, you need to summarize actions and commitments to next steps. You confirm alignment on the issue and then you both confirm your commitment to the solution."

"OK, so I outline what we've agreed upon and then make a plan for a resolution?"

"Yes, and you have to repeat back to the other person what you both agree is the issue and the steps you need to take to resolve it. All the while, making sure you involve the other person by asking for their input before your own and actively and mindfully listening."

"OK, you've said that a couple of times—about listening

mindfully—so I'm guessing I won't be successful without it."

"Correct! You can use all of these techniques, but if you are not truly listening to the other person, they won't be in alignment with you or fully committed to a solution, as they won't feel that you've heard their side of the story. So you confirm your alignment and commitment to the solution."

"Agreed."

"OK, so at the risk of sounding somewhat repetitive, you have to be sure to confirm that you and your meeting partner are on the same page and willing to implement the solutions or ideas. I would say this a hundred times if I had to because this part is so important and is often missed. I can tell you that if you miss this step, you won't have closure on the issue. This is where most discussions fall apart. Each person assumes that the other understands what the next steps are because they discussed it in the brainstorming step."

"Why is that?"

"Because this is where the connection point is—it's where you and the other person become aligned on the issue instead of at odds with one another."

"So it's like you're joining forces. We're all in this together, sort of thing."

"That's right... Now, one thing to keep in mind here is

that, in some cases, you may not always achieve full commitment, as there are times when this is just not possible. But if you use the six steps, you will move toward achieving a mutual and respectful understanding as we discussed earlier. There may be times when it means that you have to let go of an issue where agreement cannot be reached. It might also mean choosing to adopt the wishes of the other person—even if we do not completely agree with them or they do not agree with us."

"Right. I'm sure there are some instances where full agreement is just not possible. But at least this process offers me a much better approach to these types of conversations—and a better chance for alignment."

"Exactly. Now, the last step is also crucial: follow-up. You both agree on a date and time to follow up on the outcome of your meeting. If, at this juncture, you fail to do this, it might get forgotten in the myriad things that happen in any given week. So be sure to set a date and time together before you conclude the meeting." The beauty of this is, if for any reason the solutions that the two of you agree upon are not working, you already have a meeting set up to discuss it. If things are working, you also have the meeting set up to thank Jake for his efforts. Either way, you win!"

"Makes sense."

◆

Flora nodded. "Right. Finally, in this last step, be sure to end the meeting as you began it—with gratitude. You thank the person for meeting with you, for their input and ideas that contributed to a solution. You are also letting them know that the issue has a significant impact on both of you and you are grateful they are contributing to the outcome both parties desire."

"Plus, it's also maintaining self-regard."

"Good job, Carl—you're right. Remember to practice the gratitude exercise until you meet with Jake, and ideally, just prior to your conversation with him. Do I have your commitment to give this a try?"

"Yes, I promise..." Carl paused and looked out the window before continuing. "I wonder..."

"What's that, Carl?"

"I haven't told you about this, but...I think I'd like to."

"We still have some time...what is it?"

"Well, I've been estranged from my dad for many years now, and he has stage 4 lymphoma. He's not doing too well."

"Oh, I'm so sorry, Carl."

"Thanks. Some things were said the last time we saw each other...unforgiveable things..." But under the circumstances, I think I might regret it if I don't do something."

"Are you considering reconciling with him?"

"Well, doing this work together has made me think about him—and our relationship. And I've been journaling about it too. Today's work makes me think there could be a glimmer of hope that I might be able to handle seeing him, and I'm wrestling with the idea of talking to him again...maybe. I'm not a hundred percent sure if I can put aside my anger and resentment. But if I could, and I use these techniques, I'm thinking it could be possible."

"I think you can reconcile with your father, no question, Carl. You've gotten to the point where you're not shirking blame for your part, and you've learned new skills to deal with high-stakes situations. Just look at what happened last night with Sam. I agree with you wholeheartedly that if you don't at least try to resolve matters with your father, you could regret it."

Flora sat back in her chair and took a deep breath, then continued. "Sometimes a past mistake is a useful growth opportunity in the ongoing self-improvement project called life." She smiled. "The thing is, if you possess the wisdom—and the tools—to change things for the better, then taking action may not only bring you more inner peace, it could also motivate you to transform your other relationships. What do you think?"

"I think you're right, Flora...and I think I need to try."

◆

It finally felt like spring. Warmer days and cool nights meant no more snow—and no threat of ice storms. As Carl drove home from his office that evening, a thin, opalescent haze of frost remained over the skyline above the undulating river roadway. Around every corner the trees emerged, an unending outline of purplish gray in the waning light, and a thin ribbon of pink streaked across the sky. It was like a painting, rendered in indescribable colors. It was tranquil, motionless, and wanting for nothing. Carl met that same sense of inner calm with open arms. It was as though he held a cleverly guarded secret, one that would help him lay the foundation for a new day that was so clearly on the horizon.

# CHAPTER TEN

JAKE WAS PACING BACK AND forth in front of the conference room, his anxiety apparent in his hand movements—it looked like he was flicking water away from wet fingers. He was stewing about Carl and the last few times they'd met to discuss project issues. Jake was literally seething with clenched teeth thinking about it.

*Ugh...another meeting with him...I can't stand this guy... he's always so pompous! He thinks he knows everything! And every time I try to tell him what needs to happen, he doesn't listen. I don't care anymore! I'm not backing down...and I'm going to Ines after our meeting today to give her an earful. I've had enough!*

Somehow, Carl's office building looked more inviting that day—he wasn't sure why. It could be the season and the accompanying feeling of renewal that persisted throughout the day. The beautiful green on the trees beginning to leaf out and the cool, fresh spring air when he opened the car windows—it was all encompassing. Carl smiled to himself as he pulled into the parking lot. He paused after he turned off the engine, just for a moment, and found himself still whistling to the song that had been playing on the radio.

In that instant, he realized what was to come and felt a sickly quiver of butterflies. *Deep breaths.* It was just a talk with Jake. A simple one-on-one. Nothing more. The six steps and the four emotional management techniques would definitely sustain him this time.

*OK, let's do this!* He opened the door and ran up the stairs.

The boardroom was a little warm as the morning sun streamed through the windows. Jake had sat down with a coffee in anticipation of his meeting with Carl and was already uncomfortable.

"Hey, it's kind of warm in here, isn't it?" Carl offered, as he strode through the doors of the conference room.

"Yeah, I guess," Jake grumbled.

"I think I'll turn down the heat a bit and maybe leave the

doors open—OK for you?"

Jake turned to look at Carl and shrugged as Carl was putting the doorstop on one of the heavy plate-glass doors and wondered why he was suddenly being so considerate.

"Jake, I want to thank you for meeting with me this morning. I know you are really busy over in Production."

"Whatever, Carl. Can we just get this over with? I have a lot on my plate and I don't want to waste time. We never seem to get anywhere anyway," he said sarcastically. "And you always seem to have all the answers, right?"

Carl laughed slightly, but it was interesting to him that he didn't feel anger rising up. Instead, he just felt...neutral. He knew the stress Jake was under and now understood why he was on the defensive. Jake needed the opportunity to speak his mind, and Carl wanted his participation in the solution. He paused briefly to take a deep breath before continuing. "Listen. Jake...I know you have a very difficult job trying to keep on top of all the demands that are put upon your department—and I think it's pretty admirable that you are able to handle all that. It can't be easy. You have people to manage plus all of us in Sales making somewhat unreasonable demands—you have a very problematic job."

*What's he up to...?* Jake wondered. He hesitated for a

moment and then retorted, "Well, it would be nice if someone would actually *listen to me* once in a while."

"Yes, I'm sure that's true. OK, the reason I wanted to meet with you again is to discuss how we can get past some of the issues we are having, like the late deliveries. I'd like to talk this through to see where I could help. And I want you to know, I take full responsibility for my part in all of the challenges we've had." Carl paused for a moment before continuing. "You know, it might help me to better understand your department. I want to do what I can to be aware of the issues—and how we might work together to make things run smoother, at the very least, from the orders end of things. You are the production expert, of course."

Jake was dumbfounded but began to answer cautiously. "Well...er...I was thinking maybe there have been issues because we don't have an efficient system, a set of checks and balances between Sales and Production. I think we may have to work on a new logistics structure—and I have been trying to get the owners to spring for a new tempering oven and a robotic glass-moving system. I have to rely on the guys in the plant to get things moving, and when the machines are down or one of them is sick or off, everything slows down."

Carl paused once more. In the past, he would have exploded

at this comment. Instead, he took a moment once again for a deep breath and averted his eyes to a print on the wall before continuing. "Wow, Jake, I can really see how this could affect your ability to deliver on time and how there are many variables to deal with. And that places a lot of pressure on you and your department. Does that sound right?"

Jake let out a whoosh of air. "I'll say…and I can't seem to get the message through to anyone that things have to change."

Carl leaned forward and looked straight at Jake. "Why don't we devise a plan together? If we present a united front, maybe we'll have a better chance. Do you think that might help?"

"Well, yeah, it might. It's worth a try. And honestly, Carl, I just don't think I can continue this way. It's getting so stressful—I'm ready to explode half the time," Jake revealed.

"Let's put some ideas together on paper—what do you think? We could brainstorm our approach and then plan on how we will present it. We won't be coming to them with a problem; we'll be offering a solution that might enhance production, allowing them to realize better sales, and therefore, profits. Does that sound like a plan, Jake? I really think we can make this work, as a team."

"Well sure, like I said, it's worth a try. OK, so can you research the cost of the capital equipment for me? I have to work out the layout and workflow systems, which will take a fair bit of time."

"I'd be happy to do that. Just send me the machine model numbers you are interested in, and I'll call the manufacturers' reps to see what, if any, discounts they might offer—particularly if we do a package deal. We'll have to be sure to show the owners we've thought it through from every angle, including cost per square foot and the potential manpower savings of going forward with the robotic solution."

The two men continued to brainstorm ideas. Ines walked by and could hear murmurs of their discussion in the boardroom through the open door.

*Is that a friendly tone of voice...a slight laugh? What's going on in there?*

*Amazing...*

Ines realized she had stopped dead in her tracks near the boardroom—she was flabbergasted. She then turned and walked back toward her office.

Carl and Jake were wrapping up their discussion. "OK so, Jake, we both have our marching orders. When is realistic for us to get together again? Would one week be possible?"

"Yes, I don't want this to go on any longer. I'm getting so fed up with what's going on I want a solution ASAP. Let's meet next

◆

Thursday—around this time?"

"Perfect, sounds great. I'll have everything ready for you, Jake, and then we can work out our presentation. I really appreciate you taking the time today. I feel a lot better about this, and I understand where you're coming from now. I feel pretty bad that I didn't ask sooner."

"Well...I didn't tell you, either, so I guess we're both to blame." Jake smiled slightly.

◆

Carl walked down the hall to Ines' office, feeling relieved and surprisingly coolheaded. He hadn't realized the challenges Jake was facing on a daily basis. No wonder he felt under the gun all the time.

He saw Ines engrossed in reading some specifications and knocked on the glass. "Can I come in?"

"Sure thing! Take a seat." She smiled.

Carl sank into a chair. "Great. I just wanted to say thank you."

"For...?"

"For all you've done for me. I just finished a meeting with Jake, and as a result of all the work I've done with Flora, I feel like everything is so much easier. It's like a new way of communicating has opened up for me, and it's so…empowering. But the best part is, I feel so at ease. And I never really realized just how wound up I was—*all* the time. I began to recognize—from my personal profile—that I was constantly driving myself and others toward results *as I saw things*. I was pushing everyone toward consensus without stepping back… without taking the time to listen mindfully. I've been using different approaches to respond back, and it really makes a big difference. The communication skills have helped me at home, too."

Ines beamed. "Oh, Carl, I'm so happy for you! That's terrific. You do look more relaxed! You know, I must confess, I heard the sound of you two talking as a walked by the conference room a while ago…you had the door propped open."

"Yeah, it was hot in there this morning."

"Right…you know, I couldn't hear *what* you were saying, only your tones of voice—and I think I even heard a laugh exchanged between you two! What a difference from the way it used to be a couple of months ago!"

"I know…like I said, I'm really grateful to you for the opportunity. It's helped me and Jake work together on a resolution to our ongoing woes—I'll be sure to fill you in on everything as we get closer to a final solution."

◆

"Sounds like a plan, Carl."

◆

What a picture-perfect day... Carl could smell the lilacs that had burst forth in the past week as he drove past the beautiful homes in Oak Park with his sunroof open. The heady scented white, pale mauve and deep purple bushes were everywhere. They were so extraordinarily perfumed, almost intoxicating in their aroma. These beautiful moments of renewal seemed even more treasured than other spring seasons. It had been such a grueling season...a cruel fact of nature that winter had retained its grip on the city for longer than usual.

Carl pulled into Joe's driveway to see a massive circular planter at the crest of the path. It was filled with white Mandevilla flower vines, entangled on twisted willow branches that were accented by bright green ferns and variegated ivy. A large vintage Buddha head was placed in the center of the planter, a beloved sentry for its floral finery. It almost took his breath away.

As he walked to the front door, he could see Joe crouched down over a garden bed, weeding.

"Well, hello, Mr. Green Thumb!"

"Hey there! I'd shake your hand, Carl, but I'm a little mucky

◆

at the moment." Joe smiled. Let's go in—I made some iced tea lemonade."

"Sounds good, Joe. You know, I think you might need to write a cookbook—or a book on gardening. That's an incredible Buddha planter out front. Outstanding!"

"Thanks, my friend; it's sort of like creating a living canvas—I get so much joy from it. But the weeds are not my friends." He laughed. "Go on in and take a seat. I'm just going to do a quick-change act and I'll be right down."

"OK, Joe, thanks. I can't stay long, but I just wanted to talk for a bit. I'm on my way to see my dad, actually."

"Wow, really? That's fantastic, Carl! I'm so pleased! OK, hold that thought and I'll be right there!"

Carl sat in the kitchen looking at the multiple bird feeders and hummingbird stations in the back garden. It was a beautiful sight—the apple blossoms were a stunning backdrop for all the activity of hummers and other birds that were zooming from branch to branch.

Joe walked briskly into the kitchen and poured two glasses of tea with lemonade over ice. "So tell me, when did you decide to see your dad?"

"It was during a session with my coach, actually. Since I've learned all of these techniques and communication skills, I've really gained confidence—like I can get through it, you know? I had a meeting with that guy at work I told you about too..."

"Jake?"

"The very same. Now that I've implemented these techniques, I'm able to talk to him—and even come to alignment on difficult issues. I've discovered that I'm not stuck in the same communication rut. By regulating my emotions, I can adjust my approach. I can even be more candid, and I'm able to let go and shift to being a better listener. Maybe that's all Jake really wanted—for me to listen to him." Carl thought for a moment before going on. "The things I've learned in sessions have even helped me at home, talking to Sam and Maria. I'm feeling so much more...in the moment, as you would say." Carl chuckled. "I told you I've been meditating too, right?"

"Yes, you mentioned that. I'd definitely be in bad shape without my practice, I can tell you that..."

"And I've been journaling and doing this gratitude exercise—it's all been quite the transformation. I'm so grateful for the experience."

"So you've reached a point where you can forgive yourself and others, I take it? And that means your father is next on the list. I'm so happy for you, Carl. So, what did you want to talk to me about?"

◆

"Well, I guess I'm just looking for moral support. I'm a little nervous. Any pearls of wisdom for me?"

Joe looked out the window for a moment and then turned to face Carl. "Be selfish about it."

"What…? What are you talking about? I thought I was being…oh, I don't know…benevolent…unselfish…openhearted…by forgiving him," Carl stammered.

"You are."

"What do you mean by selfish?"

"You are in the process of learning to forgive…others as well as yourself. You've already noticed what's happening. You're feeling better—lighter and calmer, correct?"

"Yes, absolutely."

"Have you noticed any other positive changes?"

"Well, it's interesting. I notice people seem to be nicer, or warmer. I'm not sure how to put it… Maybe it's because I'm less stressed around them."

"That and the fact that you now know how to communicate with them with grace and wisdom."

"OK, so where's the selfish part?"

"That's easy, Carl. Do you want more of the same? Do you want to develop even better relationships and feel like you are more fulfilled? In terms of your father, imagine how good it

◆

will feel to go to sleep at night, knowing that you extended a hand—in peace—to him. That you are able to let go of the past, and more importantly, that you are able to let go of how he may have wronged you and simply show him love. Go after that sense of freedom—it's such a blessing. That sense of peace…be selfish about it." Joe smiled warmly.

"You are amazing, Joe. I'm so lucky to have you in my life. Thanks, I think I'm ready to go over there now."

"Be sure to let me know how it goes, Carl." Joe reached over and squeezed Carl's shoulder. "I know you can do this. Just speak with love in your heart and forgiveness in your soul."

"Thanks for everything, Joe."

◆

His heart rate was racing as Carl drove past the homes in the old neighborhood. His primary school, the corner store and the burger joint in the strip mall were all that remained of the relics of his youth. So much had changed, even in the few years he had not been back.

Carl pulled into the gravel drive and got out. His heart was pounding as he walked up the front path. The house looked a little disregarded and in need of some TLC. The stucco needed to be repaired, there were weeds popping up everywhere, even the grass was overgrown…

*This place needs some love…*

He rang the bell.

A tall woman in pastel-blue scrubs answered the door. "Hello, you must be Carl," she said, smiling warmly. "I spoke to you on the phone the other day."

"Right. You mentioned this might be a good time to come by?"

"Yes, your father has just had his dinner and his last dose of medication before bedtime—so he should be just fine. I did tell him you were coming, though; I hope you don't mind. I didn't think it would be a good idea to surprise him, in his condition."

"Oh, no, absolutely. You're right—I didn't think of that. How's he doing today?"

"Well, he takes each day as it comes. I know he's lonely though, so I'm glad you're here. He's been asking what time you were coming all day. Go on inside, dear."

Carl could hear the pump of an oxygen machine as he rounded the corner in the hallway. He could see the pale light of the evening coming through the dark curtains in his dad's room, and he almost gasped at the sight. His father was so frail, so small, almost childlike. The sight of him in his ailing, weakened state alarmed Carl, but he moved toward the bed and sat down next to his father.

They sat in silence together for what seemed to Carl like an eternity. His eyes wandered from his dad to the family photos in the room and on to the burgeoning buds on the trees outside the window. It was such a beautiful day.

He looked down at his father; his eyes were tracing Carl's face as if he were trying to memorize every inch. It was as though he was searching for something—maybe a sign that Carl could find it in his heart to forgive him. His father seemed to be already retreating...disappearing...to somewhere remote and inaccessible.

Carl felt a pang of anxiety. Grief swamped him suddenly, tearing at his heart and gripping the pit of his stomach. It was as though he was cast out to sea, caught in an enormous wave that was rolling over him. He focused on his breathing, slowly in and out, to calm himself.

His father tried to speak between labored breaths. "Son...I hope...you know..."

Tears welled up in Carl's eyes, but he tried to contain himself, fixing his gaze on the vista outside the bedroom window. He swallowed hard. Reaching over the edge of the bed, he took his father's hand; it was so thin and pale, almost transparent. He placed his dad's hand between his and gently squeezed it.

◆

"Dad...I really...need...to talk to you..." Carl struggled with the words as he fought to hold back the tears.

His dad looked up at him and whispered words Carl had not heard from his father in a very long time.

"I love you, Son."

# ADDENDUM:
## THE SCIENCE BEHIND MEANINGFUL ALIGNMENT

THE MANY CHALLENGES THAT OUR story's protagonist, Carl, experienced in the pursuit of alignment and harmony in his personal and professional relationships are common for many people. We wrote this story because it reflects the communication and relationship challenges that we see all around us in the world today, but more specifically, it is also what we've observed for years through our executive coaching practice and leadership development projects.

Despite the daunting problems that business leaders are facing as they work to build and maintain a collaborative culture, they are also identifying some powerful solutions—most

◆

notably, the need to select, develop and promote future leaders based on emotional intelligence as a key competency. One company after another has been adding interpersonal communication training to their emerging leadership programs, as well as mindfulness programs, yoga, exercise rooms and nutritious lunch options. In essence, we see Meaningful Alignment as an extension of these efforts to focus on the emotional, mental and physical well-being of employees.

Over the course of the past twelve years of debriefing emotional intelligence test results with our executive coaching clients, we also began to recognize some common themes and patterns emerging; evidence that many of our clients were struggling in the same areas: (1) underestimating the power that emotions have when seeking to influence people, (2) overestimating their ability to control and regulate their own emotions as well as shape the emotional responses of others, and (3) failing to invest the time necessary to prepare for emotional labor or to recover from emotional strain.

Practically speaking, these problems show up in the concrete issues they routinely face:

- How can I maintain team cohesion when everything around me is changing constantly and moving so quickly?
- How can I achieve work-life balance in the age of the

smartphone, where people expect to have access to me around the clock?
• Why do so many people I work with, including leaders above me, fail to hold one another accountable in crucial moments?
• Why are people hesitant to truly tell me what they are thinking?
• Why do I feel like the harder I work this week, the more hours I'll end up working next week?

We believe that many of the socio-emotional problems we see in the world around us end up impacting the workplace. Just consider some of the challenges that coworkers come into contact with if they work on even a moderately large team. We see all of the following on the rise:
• children on medication for ADHD
• obesity across a large percentage of the population
• political division (It is hard to escape this, try as we may)
• school shootings and violence; more schools adding metal detectors and conducting regular evacuation drills
• addiction to smartphones; lack of social interaction at work and at home
• workplace aggression; workplace bullying

◆

- domestic abuse
- sexual harassment
- cyber-bullying
- high turnover and frequent changes to job responsibilities
- reorganizations, mergers and the threat of layoffs
- constantly changing technology
- elimination of privacy; reduced perceptions of safety and security
- work-related emails and texts outside of regular business hours
- increased road rage incidents in high-growth urban and suburban areas
- increased rate of diagnosis for depression and anxiety disorders
- increased reliance on medication and the many side effects of prescriptions
- increased reliance on processed food and fast food (a direct result of working long hours, day after day)

You get the gist of the problems people face. Today we live in a hyper-achievement society, a society where people are forced to process a constantly and rapidly changing world. A generation ago, the world of work consisted of a much higher percentage of noncognitive, repetitive, predictable tasks. This sense of predictability, and the routine "ritual" aspects of work gave our minds and our emotions (our nervous systems) periods of respite throughout the day. Furthermore, people were able to more readily decompress at the end of the work day. Cell phones were rare, and call minutes were expensive, so people were not constantly plugged-in, tuned-in, and bathing their eyes in the stimulating light of a phone screen. As a result, people found adequate time and space each day to regulate their mental and emotional lives.

The old paradigm has changed radically. The vast majority of work tasks that consisted of patterned decision-making or repetition are almost entirely automated by software algorithms. This has pushed the performance expectations and the type of work for most jobs (especially higher-salary jobs) toward tasks that have high cognitive and emotional demand and very little task repetition. This increases the amount of stress being absorbed per day and per hour. Time has also collapsed in many workplaces. Managers are often pressed to go beyond the normal strategic planning work and are now engaged in relentless "pre-mortem" exercises, where they are tasked with predicting everything that could possibly go wrong in the future and

◆

then must work backward to continually plan, prepare, prevent and execute. It can be an excellent exercise for leaders to use with their teams, but it is exhausting and stressful when the exercise never seems to end because the rules of the marketplace keep changing.

Finally, we've also observed that many managers (and employees alike) have lost the art of face-to-face management and interpersonal communication. The ubiquitous use of smartphone technology is partly to blame for this, especially the heavy reliance on texting (even when the recipient is just down the hall). As a result, information that does get communicated is typically light on personal substance and heavy on tasks, interruptions and busy work. The difficult and time-sensitive conversations that need to occur are simply not happening up and down the organization, and whenever these discussions do occur, the substance of what really needs to be said is rarely addressed. We recall one marketing executive that we were assisting who was hoping to use his hourly coaching sessions to help him prepare for a long-promised promotion to senior vice president. However, unbeknownst to him (and to us too, until it was too late!), his boss was actually in the process of terminating him. We wish that this type of wild disconnect between people was a rare occurrence, but it seems to be far more commonplace than it used to be.

As a result of our years of observation and coaching experience, we decided take action on the problem. To begin, we embarked on a journey to collect data. Lots of data. We began by combing through the many records of past coaching engagements. We created numerous assessments and hundreds of behavior-based survey items. We reworked one iteration after another of test instruments and conducted multiple rounds of feedback interviews and validity tests with field experts, professionals, and trusted colleagues who were willing to give us their time. Eventually, we began to see something really special emerging from the ashes of all our discarded survey items and models—a pattern between the way people experience the inner world of their feelings and beliefs (the inside game) and the external world of how they tend to communicate and interact with one another (the outside game). A set of discrete dialogue styles emerged from the data mountain with clarity, as well as a model; a circular model that was, curiously enough, very similar to some very old structural models of personality referred to as a circumplex (see figure 1).

Through this new circular model, we were able to capture how the character of one's outwardly expressed behavior was likely influenced by the intensity of their inward experience

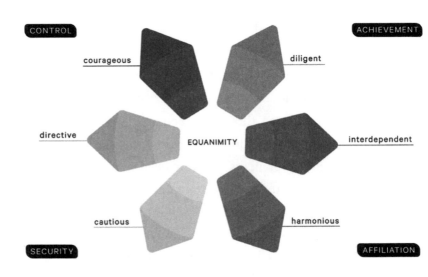

**FIGURE 1. THE INTERPERSONAL DIALOGUE PROFILE™ MODEL**

(the intensity of their positive and negative affect.) We also began to collect research on how mindfulness and gratitude practices were useful to self-regulate the "volume" of our affect and the "valence" of our mood states (positive/negative). That was an instructive connection to have made. We knew that, after all this time and effort, we were finally onto something that we could use to really benefit the lives of our clients. Our pilot research study of the assessment, the Interpersonal Dialogue Profile™, was based on a convenience sample (N=204) of adult participants. At that time, we tested eight dialogue style factors (we had predicted that our data patterns would follow previous circumplex models), but a principle component analysis helped us to reduce the model to six dialogue styles and four mental model factors.

## The Four Mental Models

To unpack the Meaningful Alignment graphic model, it is first important to describe the four higher order factors depicted on the perimeter. These mental model factors represent robust personal schemas that are shaped throughout our life, typically by our most important—and often most traumatic—life experiences. Over time, these mental models serve as guides for how to interpret current and future dilemmas, and they become the well-worn paths of our expressed social behavior. These schemas are powerful coping mechanisms that usually serve us extremely well throughout our life. Three of the mental model factors have existed for decades in various forms, most notably in the work of McClelland (1961) and other behavioral scientists via motivational theories, but we also uncovered a fourth factor—Security. In addition, we identified many practical details of how these mental model factors operate by exploring the reams of qualitative data we had collected. One important

◆

discovery, was how our most dominant motivation model will impact the language we use, the emotional responses we tend to reveal, and the semiconscious agendas we carry into each social interaction. The four mental model factors are defined below:

1. **Control**. The extent to which individuals attempt to fulfill their desires, values, principles and concerns. Interactions with others are focused on influencing, motivating and using power, to convince others to align with the preferred goals and vision. The stronger this mental model dimension is, the more likely we are to have strong emotional reactions centered around our values and/or our personal needs and desires. Others may view strong control behaviors as forceful, confrontational and inflexible.

2. **Achievement**. The extent to which individuals focus their energy and attention on solving problems, making progress toward goals and resolving differences between people objectively and rationally. Relationships and interactions with others are often described through a practical, utilitarian lens. The stronger this mental model dimension is, the more likely we are to have strong emotional reactions to obstacles, delays, distractions and disengaged persons. Others may view strong achievement behaviors as exhausting and relentless.

3. **Affiliation**. The extent to which individuals are focused on maintaining relationships. Energy is spent to ensure that people are reasonably satisfied with each interaction that transpires, even if this means altering one's own preferences to better match the needs of others or to prevent strife and conflict. Outcomes are judged by external validation. The stronger this mental model dimension is, the more likely we are to have strong emotional reactions to avoid arguments and disagreements. Those with a strong affiliation drive are likely to judge people in disagreement or engaging in acts of defiance as stubborn, cold, counterproductive and unwilling to compromise or build consensus. Others may perceive strong affiliation behaviors as signs of passivity, detachment and disengagement.

4. **Security**. The extent to which individuals are focused on self-protection, risk mitigation, and asserting boundaries. Trust is earned over time, and until it is established, outcomes geared toward protecting the best interests of one's self, family, friends, boss, department, etc., are of paramount importance. Those dominant in this model have an emotionally guarded nature, aimed at avoiding time and energy-wasting social behaviors that cause undue stress, disputes and counterproductive disagreements. The stronger this mental model dimension is, the more likely we are to have strong emotional reactions

to behaviors perceived as threatening or manipulative. Others may view strong security behaviors as elusive, protective, defensive and self-serving.

## The Six Dialogue Styles

It is important to think of the mental model framework itself as only wielding very high-level influences in our communication style. Rather than testing for them directly, the mental models are revealed through the patterned emergence of six distinct dialogue styles. These lie at the heart of the model and provide the foundation for the Interpersonal Dialogue Profile™. They are defined as follows:

The **Directive** style is characterized by feelings that are bold, competitive and certain. We use this approach when we give orders, make our demands known and provide directions. In its most balanced form, the internal feeling is one of assertiveness. As an example, we can all think of times when others have relied on us to take charge and provide clarity, and we can likely recall the emotions we felt. However, the more intense these feelings are, the less likely (and/or less often) the feeling will prove useful. We can allow competitive feelings and the desire to "win" to overshadow the more positive aspects of this style when it is centered on the confidence of our knowledge, vision and experience.

The **Courageous** style is characterized by fearlessness and daring. When balanced, this style helps us to overcome fear, and to align our words and actions with a sense of integrity, purpose, and meaning. The Courageous style provides the drive necessary for us to intervene, take on the role of the whistle-blower and overcome the social conformity of groupthink. The natural, nervy feeling we often experience in these situations requires daring and confidence—that is, a feeling of overcoming fears and taking action based on integrity, safety, obligation and duty. When the feeling is significantly out of balance, we can become a destructive force in the name of principle, or become blinded by our own faith in our sense of what is best, perhaps to the point that we aren't able to maintain our objectivity or keep an open mind.

The **Diligent** style is characterized by truth-seeking and problem-solving. When balanced, the internal feelings associated with this style lead us to a laser-focused mindset aimed at attaining goals and solving problems. We use this approach with others in many ways: discussing the legality of a business decision, determining the highest-quality product or deducing the most logical or soundest way to proceed. Driven by the Diligent style, we channel all our emotional energies toward thought, reason, deduction and analysis rather than to the relationships with those involved in our collaborative ventures. When this approach becomes very intense and out of balance, we can utterly exhaust ourselves and others. We insist on turning over every rock in the garden until the issues are hashed out and resolved and closure is obtained. If we cannot agree on the best outcome, we risk gaining false consensus through frustration, or we "agree to disagree." The inability to let go, in this case, creates a feeling that the agreement may not have been worth the intense effort required to achieve it. People can also be left feeling as though they represented little more than a means to an end.

The **Interdependent** style is characterized by a spirit of collaboration and a desire to achieve consensus-based outcomes with others, based on a win-win attitude. Whereas the Diligent approach is concerned with the utility of interactions, the Interdependent approach is concerned with the satisfaction of relationships, commitments and agreements. Being right or "winning" is a victory only when all parties involved feel victorious. In this style's most balanced form, we remain interested and curious about the needs of other people, and we invite others to understand our own needs in equal measure. When two or more people are committed to this approach, a tremendous amount of work can be accomplished and breakthrough agreements realized. However, if feelings are intense and out of balance, we can overvalue consensus and become attached to satisfying the needs of all parties involved. This can lead to disappointments, analysis paralysis, misconceptions about the purpose of engagements and an inefficient use of effort and time.

The **Harmonious** style is characterized by a desire to fulfill the needs of others. This approach is positive when based on acts of selfless love, admiration and trust. It can be counterproductive when we aren't capable of standing up for our own needs or when we acquiesce to the will of others even when their desires aren't sound or smart. When adopting this style, we can be effective servant-leaders and exceptional team players, and we develop highly conscientious instincts. However, if we allow this style to be a dominant approach to interaction, we risk developing feelings of resignation and even resentment at being taken advantage of. We can also frustrate other people in our lives by frequent emotional check-in behaviors and the need for external validation.

The **Cautious** style is characterized by unknown or low degrees of trust. These are the feelings we encounter when we believe it is vital to "trust but verify." Low-to-moderate levels of trust lead us to demand proof ("I will believe it when I see it"). We feel this way when our goal is to protect our positions in a negotiation or discussion. Compromise and quid-pro-quo tactics are often the go-to approach. As a result, we show others only one card at a time, and we tend to wait and see what the other party wants before we will reveal all of our hidden needs. This is a common situation people experience on car sales lots, when dealing with people we don't know, or in salary negotiations with a potential employer. When this style is balanced, we use it to give and receive information carefully, skeptically and methodically. We use it to ensure we are maintaining objectivity, limiting our vulnerability, constraining excitement and keeping our expectations realistic. We also adopt this style when we seek to protect ourselves from overcommitment. This allows us to "under-promise and over-deliver" on the things most important to us. When this style is out of balance, an overly cautious nature may lead us to be highly guarded, unreasonably skeptical and closed; we may also be inclined to presume that other people or parties involved are trying to take advantage of us. When the lack of trust in someone is intense, it can cause us to completely disregard communication or, perhaps, to cut ties entirely.

In order to see how a pattern of scores along the six dialogue styles may indicate one or more dominant mental model factors, it is best to visualize it through a radar (or spider) graph of a sample assessment result. This can be seen through figure 2.

The radar graph in figure 2 reveals one clear mental model. The mental model framework itself emerged from our early data collection efforts, consisting of boss, peer, and direct report interview transcripts (commonly referred to as multi-rater interviews). Coaching clients with a dialogue pattern similar to the results illustrated in figure 2 will exhibit communication traits, habits and emotional responses to social situations—without fail—that align with the Achievement mental model. The most common mental models associated with the Achievement domain in our transcript data are as follows:

- Working hard is how I know that I am valuable.
- I must exceed expectations.
- A person is either part of the solution or part of the problem.
- Results speak for themselves.
- Never start something you cannot finish.

As mentioned, our mental models function as cognitive scripts that lead us to form belief statements—often unconsciously—about ourselves, the motives of other people, and the world in which we live. A dominant mental model helps us to

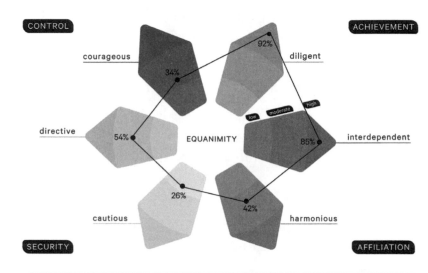

**FIGURE 2. SAMPLE PROFILE PATTERN—HIGH ACHIEVEMENT MENTAL MODEL**

thrive and often leads us to tremendous levels of success. As a consequence, however, mental models can also dominate how we interpret our world, and over time, they can become limiting and oppressive. In relationships at work and at home, our mental models can become an oppressive force that prevents us from truly flourishing. From our Achievement mental model example, the following challenges routinely emerge in our multi-rater (interview) transcript data:

**TABLE 1.** Mental Model Challenges

| Mental Model (Achievement) | Challenges |
|---|---|
| • Working hard is how I know that I am valuable.<br><br>• I must exceed expectations. | Poor work-life balance; demotivates team members by modeling unrealistic, unsustainable examples. Overcommits; says yes to too many initiatives; feels distressed if left out of any important projects. |
| • A person is either part of the solution or part of the problem.<br><br>• Results speak for themselves. | Strong judgments of others related to perceived outcomes; people are unconsciously viewed as a means to an end, leading to superficial, transactional relationships. |
| • Never start something you cannot finish. | Cannot easily let go of unfinished business. Compulsive communication habits; mental rumination of problems. Can lead to perfectionism, micromanagement, and the need for inclusion on every detail of a project. |

Although these challenging behaviors seldom take a person by surprise when they come face-to-face with them, people with the Achievement mental model rarely consider just how deep these compulsive patterns go or how misguided or exaggerated their underlying core beliefs are. The work ahead is to encourage these clients to be open to new beliefs, to learn to let go and reinvest their focus in different approaches and expand their capacity to self-regulate feelings that quickly trigger habitual patterns of behavior. This coaching work includes the intense practice of new skills for building Meaningful Alignment with others. We accomplish this by establishing a regular practice in mindfulness and gratitude exercises, developing targeted emotional intelligence skills (based on the client's unique set of emotional intelligence test results), and finally, by practicing the Meaningful Alignment Process (MAP) prior to engaging with key people, particularly prior to conducting a pivotal, high-stakes meeting or interaction.

## SOME TECHNICAL STUFF

### Reliability and Descriptive Statistics
For any assessment, it is important that all items that load on a specific factor be consistent across all raters (study participants).

**TABLE 2.** Central Tendency, Standard Deviation, Skewness, Kurtosis, and Reliability

| Scale | M | SD | Median | Skewness | Kurtosis | Reliability |
|---|---|---|---|---|---|---|
| Harmonious | 22.19 | 8.34 | 22.00 | .10 | -.80 | .84 |
| Cautious | 24.95 | 7.80 | 26.00 | -.27 | -.61 | .83 |
| Directive | 20.02 | 6.36 | 20.00 | .27 | .36 | .79 |
| Courageous | 23.88 | 7.98 | 23.00 | .09 | -.64 | .83 |
| Diligent | 25.54 | 6.05 | 26.00 | -.05 | -.43 | .79 |
| Interdependent | 26.33 | 6.70 | 26.00 | -.14 | -.60 | .81 |

This is referred to as external reliability. Reliability coefficients for all six dialogue factors ranged between .79 and .84. All scales in our model had distribution characteristics within standard practice and guidance, which includes skewness less than 1.0 and kurtosis less than 2.0 with respect to sample sizes in the range of our second pilot ($n = 242$). Table 2 presents each of the scales and descriptive statistics of central tendency, variability, distribution and reliability.

Once we know that individual assessment items have acceptable descriptive characteristics and reliabilities, we can examine relationships between the style factors through convergent and discriminant correlations. We do this to evaluate adequate factor independence. It is vital to recognize that human behavior is seldom pure or perfectly captured by only one factor and absent entirely of another. As a result, we actually want some factor scores to positively correlate with one another up to a point; this is particularly true for styles that reside closer to one another on the conceptual model.

Conversely, we also want to see style dimensions that are distant or opposite from one another revealing negative correlations with statistical significance, but again, only up to a point. After all, we are not measuring completely different categories (types of giraffe versus types of automobile). We are trying to capture an entire set of social behaviors that we all engage in to varying degrees depending on the context we find ourselves in. For example, even the most confrontation-averse person imaginable can, when their values are at risk of being violated, find themselves acting in a highly confrontative manner. As an illustrative example, we want to see the Diligent and Interdependent style factors exhibit at least some convergence, and indeed we did ($r = .24$, $p < .05$). We also want to see negative correlations where they are expected to emerge, for example, between the Cautious and the Courageous styles ($r = -.52$, $p < .01$). All of the relationships can be observed in the set of convergent-discriminant correlations in table 3.

**TABLE 3. Convergent-Discriminant Correlations**

|  | Harmonious | Cautious | Directive | Courageous | Diligent |
|---|---|---|---|---|---|
| **Cautious** | .54** | | | | |
| **Directive** | -.38** | -.32* | | | |
| **Courageous** | -.54** | -.52** | .30** | | |
| **Diligent** | -.36** | -.28** | -.10 | .37** | |
| **Interdependent** | .22* | -.31** | -.06 | .07 | .24** |

*$p < .05$ **$p < .01$

### Criterion Validity

We also have identified some existing constructs of theoretical importance to examine as part of an analysis of validity. In this unique circumstance, we wanted to focus our analysis on constructs that we viewed as useful for including in a learning and development program for Meaningful Alignment. To that end, we collected data (concurrently) on five measures of interest—emotional intelligence, mindfulness, positive affect intensity, negative affect intensity and physical sensitivity—to study their covariance characteristics with the six dialogue styles. In the future, we also plan to include the Big Five personality factors—openness, conscientiousness, extraversion, agreeableness and neuroticism—to establish further construct validity for the model, but at this stage of development, we focused only on constructs we believed to have high instructional and developmental value. We define each of the constructs below, followed by the correlations that each has with the six dialogue styles, presented in table 4 on page 175.

**Emotional Intelligence:** The ability to perceive, use, understand and manage one's own emotions as well as the emotions of others. For our pilot research, we used a self-reported measure, which can only denote the degree to which a person values emotional abilities and is able to accurately estimate their own behavior. We found this construct to be correlated with three styles, all of which reside in proximity on the model (Courageous, Diligent and Interdependent). As with the mindfulness construct that follows, this result does not indicate that some styles are "better" than others.

**Mindfulness:** The ability to self-regulate attention to the present moment without cognitive judgment or distractions; a frame of mind marked by a sustained attitude of openness, acceptance and curiosity. We found this construct to be positively correlated with the Interdependent dialogue style. As with emotional intelligence, this does not indicate that the Interdependent style is preferable to other styles.

**Affect Intensity:** Refers to the strength and frequency of one's feelings in response to life situations. Affect intensity refers to one overall dimension of emotional reactivity. This is further divided into aspects of "valence" (see positive and negative affect below).

**PA (Positive Affect):** The intensity by which one experiences positive feelings and reacts to environmental and social stimuli with intensely pleasant sensations. This construct was positively correlated with the Harmonious dialogue style.

**NA (Negative Affect):** The intensity by which one experiences negative feelings and reacts to environmental and social stimuli with intensely unpleasant sensations. This construct was negatively correlated with the Diligent dialogue style, meaning that when people scored higher in the Diligent style, they also tended to have somewhat lower NA scores. Conversely, the higher the person's NA score, the less likely it is that the individual will score themselves high in the Diligent style.

**Physical Sensitivity:** A short measure we developed that is closely related to highly sensitive persons, which is best understood through the work of Elaine Aron (1997). The more sensitive a person's nervous system is, the easier it is for them to become overwhelmed and saturated by the energy of their surroundings. However, they also are keener to recognize subtly in their environment, and theoretically, they are quick to rely on intuition to act or to make decisions. We found this construct to be positively related to the Cautious dialogue style. Interestingly, we also found physical sensitivity to be negatively correlated with the two boldest and most deterministic styles (Courageous and Diligent).

For some readers, a table may not be the most useful aid for visualizing how the style factors are related to one another. In order to better understand all of the convergent-discriminant relationships, we have provided figures 3 through 13 as a visual aid. Positive correlations are presented as fields of gray plus

## TABLE 4. Convergent-Discriminant Correlations: Criterion Measures of Interest

|  | Emotional Intelligence | Mindfulness | Positive Affect | Negative Affect | Affect Intensity | Physical Sensitivity |
|---|---|---|---|---|---|---|
| **Harmonious** | -.07 | -.08 | .29** | .14 | .32** | .20 |
| **Cautious** | .13 | -.10 | .18 | .10 | .12 | .26** |
| **Directive** | -.07 | -.11 | .10 | .11 | -.04 | -.11 |
| **Courageous** | .28** | .17 | .02 | -.10 | -.07 | -.23* |
| **Diligent** | .29** | .21 | -.04 | -.26** | -.16 | -.28* |
| **Interdependent** | .51** | .40** | .21 | .14 | .04 | -.16 |

*$p < .05$  **$p < .01$

signs, and negative correlations with lighter shaded fields of minus signs. When variables were not correlated, they are listed in the tables below as "(UC)" for "uncorrelated."

## FIGURE 3. CONVERGENT-DISCRIMINANT MAP: HARMONIOUS

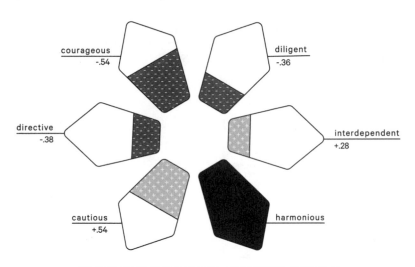

|  | Harmonious |
| --- | --- |
| Cautious | .54** |
| Directive | -.38** |
| Courageous | -.54** |
| Diligent | -.36** |
| Interdependent | .28* |

*p < .05  **p < .01

## FIGURE 4. CONVERGENT-DISCRIMINANT MAP: CAUTIOUS

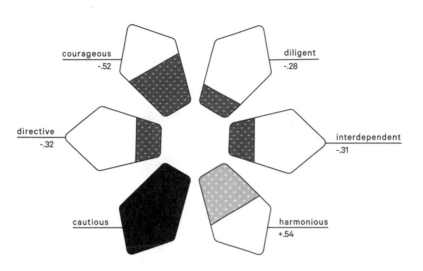

courageous
-.52

diligent
-.28

directive
-.32

interdependent
-.31

cautious

harmonious
+.54

|  | **Cautious** |
|---|---|
| Harmonious | .54** |
| Directive | -.32* |
| Courageous | -.52** |
| Diligent | -.28** |
| Interdependent | -.31** |

*p < .05  **p < .01

## FIGURE 5. CONVERGENT-DISCRIMINANT MAP: DIRECTIVE

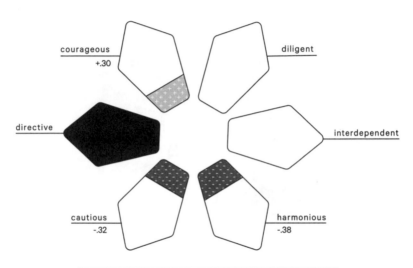

|  | **Directive** |
|---|---|
| Harmonious | -.38** |
| Cautious | -.32* |
| Courageous | .30** |
| Diligent | (UC) |
| Interdependent | (UC) |

*p < .05  **p < .01*

**FIGURE 6. CONVERGENT-DISCRIMINANT MAP: COURAGEOUS**

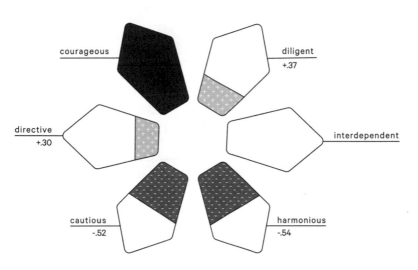

|  | Cautious |
| --- | --- |
| Harmonious | -.54** |
| Cautious | -.52** |
| Directive | .30** |
| Diligent | .37** |
| Interdependent | (UC) |

*p <.05  **p <.01

◆

## FIGURE 7. CONVERGENT-DISCRIMINANT MAP: DILIGENT

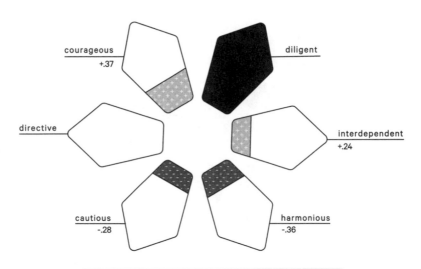

|  | Diligent |
| --- | --- |
| Harmonious | -.36** |
| Cautious | -.28** |
| Directive | (UC) |
| Courageous | .37** |
| Interdependent | .24** |

*p < .05  **p < .01

**FIGURE 8. CONVERGENT-DISCRIMINANT MAP: INTERDEPENDENT**

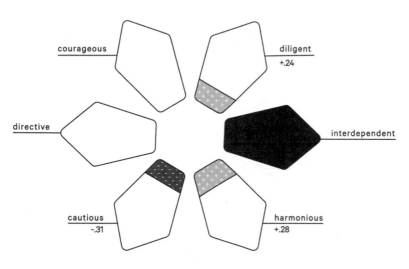

|  | Interdependent |
|---|---|
| Harmonious | .28* |
| Cautious | -.31** |
| Directive | (UC) |
| Courageous | (UC) |
| Diligent | .24** |

*p < .05  **p < .01*

◆

**FIGURE 9. CONVERGENT-DISCRIMINANT MAP: EMOTIONAL INTELLIGENCE**

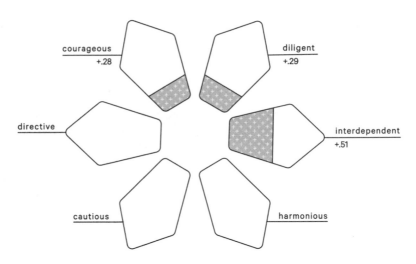

|  | **Emotional Intelligence** |
|---|---|
| Harmonious | (UC) |
| Cautious | (UC) |
| Directive | (UC) |
| Courageous | .28** |
| Diligent | .29** |
| Interdependent | .51** |

*p < .05  **p < .01*

**FIGURE 10. CONVERGENT-DISCRIMINANT MAP: MINDFULNESS**

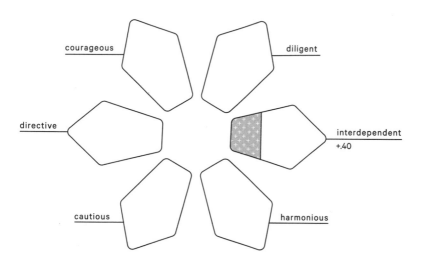

|  | **Mindfulness** |
|---|---|
| Harmonious | (UC) |
| Cautious | (UC) |
| Directive | (UC) |
| Courageous | (UC) |
| Diligent | (UC) |
| Interdependent | .40** |

*p < .05  **p < .01

**FIGURE 11. CONVERGENT-DISCRIMINANT MAP: POSITIVE AFFECT**

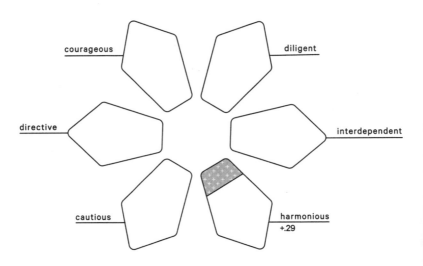

|  | **Positive Affect** |
|---|---|
| Harmonious | .29** |
| Cautious | (UC) |
| Directive | (UC) |
| Courageous | (UC) |
| Diligent | (UC) |
| Interdependent | (UC) |

*p < .05  **p < .01*

FIGURE 12. CONVERGENT-DISCRIMINANT MAP: NEGATIVE AFFECT

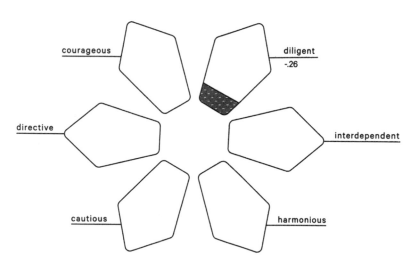

|  | **Negative Affect** |
|---|---|
| Harmonious | (UC) |
| Cautious | (UC) |
| Directive | (UC) |
| Courageous | (UC) |
| Diligent | -.26** |
| Interdependent | (UC) |

*p < .05  **p < .01

## FIGURE 13. CONVERGENT-DISCRIMINANT MAP: PHYSICAL SENSITIVITY

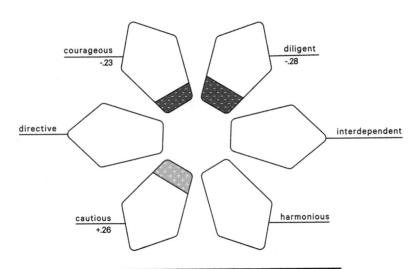

|  | Physical Sensitivity |
| --- | --- |
| Harmonious | (UC) |
| Cautious | .26** |
| Directive | (UC) |
| Courageous | -.23* |
| Diligent | -.28* |
| Interdependent | (UC) |

*p < .05  **p < .01

◆

## The Purpose of the Meaningful Alignment Program

It is important to note that we do not intend for the Interpersonal Dialogue Profile or the Meaningful Alignment program to be an exhaustive taxonomy of communication styles and traits, nor did we set out to propose a radical new theory of affect-based social interaction. The purpose of the Interpersonal Dialogue Profile is to provide users with a robust, practical, research-backed framework of easily recognizable and useful style dimensions that they could apply to their interpersonal relationships, both at work and at home. Combined with an accompanying workshop aimed at helping to improve internal self-regulation and external communication skill, participants learn how to do the following:

• Discover which dialogue styles they tend to use, particularly when the stakes are high.

• Explore the benefits of emotional self-regulation and the methods used to help us effectively regulate our moods, in tense feelings, and responses to others.

• Increase emotional resiliency and develop new emotional intelligence skills.

• Demonstrate the six steps and emotional management techniques of the Meaningful Alignment Process (MAP).

◆

The MAP is illustrated in great detail through the story of Carl and the people in his life. His coach provided Carl with a step-by-step process that allowed him to engage others in a way that magnifies the skill of mindful listening. Despite the predilection (or maybe even a hard disposition) that some may have against mindful listening, many researchers have proven that it can be taught. Furthermore, we have found through our work with organizations, that mindfulness-in-action during a discussion is of immense value to achieving outstanding outcomes and improving the satisfaction we experience in our relationships. We find that with adequate practice, the six-step process is a powerful way to automatically place us into a state of mindful listening.

## The Importance of Developing Equanimity

There is one final component of the model to discuss, and in some ways, it is perhaps the most important aspect to convey. Although the Interpersonal Dialogue Profile is a newly developed assessment tool, we have discovered its usefulness first-hand with hundreds of workshop participants. The purpose behind its creation, is to support the development of strong communication skills in people who attend the Meaningful Alignment workshops, seminars, and of course, for the readers of this book! The skills being built, however, are not merely technical or procedural. The process was designed to gradually increase the emotional well-being of those who practice the MAP technique. The MAP and the six steps provide a structure for the user to shift into a state of active and mindful listening. But there is a second, more profound competency that the process is building within the user over time: equanimity.

We define equanimity in the context of our Meaningful Alignment program as *an internal state of calm, neutral affect and composure that is maintained until the individual intentionally shifts into a useful state of emotion.* In other words, equanimity represents the ability to function as the "eye of the storm" during high-impact, high-stakes interactions with people and to remain in that state. The development of equanimity does not occur overnight, and it is much easier for some people to maintain equanimity than it is for others. This is one of the reasons why the Interpersonal Dialogue Profile™ also measures our affect intensity, including our tendency to experience positive versus negative affect, and the strength of our avoidance and engagement drives (these are all represented as supplemental scales in the profile results). For people with a natural tendency to experience their feelings intensely, additional practice and preparation is vital to realizing the pleasant reward of equanimity.

Our research on emotions and communication styles are in line with the most compelling theory of human emotion in the scientific literature today. It has been shown in lab research (Barrett 2017) that our emotions are the result of post-cognitive appraisal (that is, they are constructed from thoughts) as a series of conditioned reactions to sensations that arise in our body as pleasant and unpleasant feelings of various levels of intensity.

Consider the scenario with Carl and Jake toward the end of the story. Through some brief planning and preparation for his meeting, Carl was able to maintain a state of equanimity in the presence of his longtime workplace adversary. As a result, he was able to focus on what mattered most, which was to reach alignment with Jake on how to solve the big work challenges between them and, just as important, to establish lasting rapport. Even if Jake was completely unresponsive, it was up to Carl to determine how he would respond emotionally in kind. This is the key to the second aspect of equanimity, which is to intentionally and thoughtfully maintain emotions that are most useful. This might mean maintaining the same emotion throughout a conversation or shifting to a different emotion. The goal of equanimity is not to become an emotionless husk! The goal is to help people gain creative control

◆

of their emotional responses and choose the dialogue style that fits the needs of the situation rather than remaining hostage to emotional reactions and reverting to their most dominant dialogue style.

This is our final wish and highest purpose: to help people find joy and satisfaction in the social dimension of their lives.

# REFERENCES

Aron, Elaine N. 1997. *The Highly Sensitive Person: How to Thrive When the World Overwhelms You.* New York: Broadway Books.

Bach, Richard. 1977. *Illusions: The Adventures of a Reluctant Messiah.* New York: Dell/E. Friede.

Barrett, Lisa Feldman. 2017. *How Emotions are Made.* New York: Houghton Mifflin Harcourt.

Carstensen, Laura L. "Baby Boomers Are Isolating Themselves as They Age." *Time,* May 12, 2016. http://www.time.com/4327430.

Cross, Rob, Edward A. Madden and Scott Taylor. January 2018. "Managing Collaboration in the Workplace Efficiently." http://www.babson.edu/executive-education.

McClelland, David C. 1961. *The Achieving Society*. New York: The Free Press, A Division of Macmillan Publishing Co., Inc.

Nhat Hanh, Thich. 2014. *How to Sit*. Berkeley: Parallax Press. (paraphrased)

# ABOUT
# MEANINGFUL ALIGNMENT
## THE PROGRAM

WHAT IS WORSE THAN HAVING A high-stakes conversation? Avoiding one. Achieving Meaningful Alignment is a training program that will transform the way you and your team communicate, manage emotions and resolve conflict.

The inability to effectively handle high-stakes conversations costs organizations an enormous amount of time and money. Achieving Meaningful Alignment is a program developed by leadership experts Steinbrecher And Associates, Inc. to help individuals and teams learn how to communicate extraordinarily well and successfully build high levels of trust.

---

---------------◆---------------

A lack of alignment creates problems in the workplace such as:

- Avoidant and reactive management culture
- Team members not receiving crucial, timely feedback
- Teams and individuals not being held accountable
- Fewer innovative, creative and collaborative behaviors
- Teams ill-equipped to resolve issues and solve problems (low autonomy)

Meaningful Alignment refers to any conversation involving two or more people where alignment and deep understanding are vital to a successful outcome. More specifically, we are referring to the high stakes interactions we have at times where emotions run high, and viewpoints are often not aligned.

By our basic nature, many of us have difficulty handling emotionally charged conversations. Our capacity to manage emotions, handle conflict, and communicate authentically is not innate — it must be learned. However, few of us are trained to focus on emotional management skills throughout our careers. We have been rewarded for results, not emotional intelligence.

The secret to all successful relationships is based on mastering two aspects of emotional intelligence: the "inside game" of self-regulation and equanimity, and the "outside game" of facilitating the emotions of others.

The Achieving Meaningful Alignment program equips you and your team with a set of "tools" that will allow you to:
- Acquire the critical competencies of equanimity
- Master the techniques to engage others, skillfully, while managing emotion

Achieving Meaningful Alignment Program Highlights:
- Learn which dialogue styles we tend to use with others, particularly when the stakes are high, and disagreements are strong
- Discover vital techniques to manage your own emotions, and the emotions of others
- Explore ways to build greater emotional resiliency
- Learn and practice the six steps and emotional manage ment techniques of Meaningful Alignment
- Training programs, workshops and keynotes are available

◆

A successful and satisfying outcome for all parties involved during a discussion begins with understanding ourselves and the "inside game" of our mind. This deeper self-knowledge is achieved through our Interpersonal Dialogue Profile assessment.

**BONUS – Discover Your Personal Dialogue Style:**
Fill out our Interpersonal Dialogue Profile assessment online at meaningfulalignment.com to determine your personal dialogue style. (Please note: this offer will be available for a limited time.)

# ABOUT THE AUTHORS

**Susan Steinbrecher**
**President & CEO, Steinbrecher And Associates, Inc.**
Susan Steinbrecher, business consultant, professional speaker and licensed mediator, is president and CEO of Steinbrecher And Associates, Inc. a management consulting firm that provides professional development services in the areas of executive coaching, group facilitation, and leadership training. Susan works with senior executives and their organizations to develop and implement innovative and profit-building solutions to address the global and day-to-day challenges of leadership, operations, human resources and training.

Susan's expertise has positively impacted companies

worldwide, including Bank of America, BNSF Railway, Blue-Cross BlueShield of Tennessee, Brinker International, Capital One, Concentra, CVS Health, Delta Airlines, Marriott International, Hilton Worldwide, Miraval Spa and Resorts and Starbucks Coffee Company.

She is the coauthor of *Heart-Centered Leadership: Lead Well, Live Well* and author of the Amazon bestseller, *KENSHO: A Modern Awakening*. Susan is a regular contributor to Inc.com and her work has been featured on MSNBC's Your Business, The New York Times, Fortune Small Business, BusinessInsider.com, Entrepreneur.com HuffingtonPost.com and CNNMoney.com

## Robert Schaefer, Ph.D
### Vice President of Client Services,
### Steinbrecher And Associates, Inc.

Robert Schaefer has been with Steinbrecher And Associates, Inc. since 2005 as an Organizational Development (OD) consultant, executive coach, leadership development expert, statistical analyst, research scholar, workshop facilitator, and training systems designer. Robert is a renowned expert in the assessment and diagnostic debrief of ability-based emotional intelligence, individual and team communication styles, and the impact of mood and emotions in the workplace.

Robert has a Ph.D. in Organizational Psychology, an MBA, and is a member of the APA (American Psychological Association) and SIOP (Society for Industrial Organizational Psychology). Robert also serves as an adjunct instructor for the MBA program at the University of the People.

**Connect with us:**

meaningfulalignment.com
info@meaningfulalignment.com

# NOTES